Arthur Gay Payne

Cassell's Vegetarian Cookery

A Manual of Cheap and Wholesome Diet

Arthur Gay Payne

Cassell's Vegetarian Cookery
A Manual of Cheap and Wholesome Diet

ISBN/EAN: 9783744785075

Printed in Europe, USA, Canada, Australia, Japan

Cover: Foto ©Andreas Hilbeck / pixelio.de

More available books at **www.hansebooks.com**

CASSELL'S VEGETARIAN COOKERY.

A MANUAL OF
CHEAP AND WHOLESOME DIET.

BY

A. G. PAYNE, B.A.

AUTHOR OF "CHOICE DISHES," ETC.

CASSELL & COMPANY, Limited:
LONDON, PARIS & MELBOURNE.
1891.
[ALL RIGHTS RESERVED.]

For Puddings, Blanc-Mange, Custards,
CHILDREN'S AND INVALIDS' DIET,
And all the Uses of Arrowroot,

BROWN & POLSON'S
CORN FLOUR

HAS A WORLD-WIDE REPUTATION,
AND IS DISTINGUISHED FOR
UNIFORMLY SUPERIOR QUALITY.

NOTE.—Purchasers should insist on being supplied with BROWN & POLSON'S CORN FLOUR. Inferior qualities, asserting fictitious claims, are being offered.

80th Thousand, *price* **1s.**; *post free*, **1s. 3d.**

Cassell's Shilling Cookery.

This new and valuable Work contains 364 pages, crown 8vo, bound in limp cloth.

"This is the largest and most comprehensive work on the subject of cookery ever yet published at the price."—*Christian Age.*

"Housekeepers **will save many shillings** if they follow the practical suggestions and excellent advice given."—*Bazaar.*

"CASSELL'S SHILLING COOKERY is certainly the cheapest manual for the kitchen we have ever received. There are 360 pages of recipes, the book is serviceably bound, and should prove a treasure to any young wife."—*Weekly Times and Echo.*

CASSELL & COMPANY, LIMITED, *Ludgate Hill,* London.

[Face Preface.

PREFACE.

THE present work, though written upon strictly vegetarian principles, is by no means addressed to vegetarians only. On the contrary, we hope that the following pages of recipes will be read by that enormous class throughout the country who during the last few years have been gradually changing their mode of living by eating far *less* meat, and taking vegetables and farinaceous food as a substitute.

Where there are thousands who are vegetarians from choice, there are tens of thousands who are virtually vegetarians from necessity. Again, there is another large class who from time to time adopt a vegetarian course of diet on the ground of health, and as a means of escaping from the pains attendant on gout, liver complaint, or dyspepsia.

The class we most wish to reach, however, is that one, increasing we fear, whose whole life is one continual struggle not merely to live, but to live decently.

It may seem a strong statement, but we believe it to be a true one, that only those who have tried a strictly vegetarian course of diet know what real *economy* means. Should the present work be the means of enabling even one family to become not only better in health but richer in pocket, it will not have been written in vain.

A. G. PAYNE.

SOLIDIFIED JELLY.

By Royal Letters Patent in Great Britain and Ireland, 1888. Patented in the Dominion of Canada, 1889. Patented in France, 1889. N. S. Wales, 1889. Victoria, 1889. Other Foreign Rights reserved.

CHELSEA TABLE JELLIES.

The Inventor and Patentee, in introducing this high-class article of food, begs to warn the Public that the great success and enormous demand the CHELSEA TABLE JELLIES have obtained in Great Britain has brought many imitators on the Market. A few Stores and Grocers are offering same to the Public, no doubt for the purpose of wishing to appear cheaper, or for making extra profit. The favour for the CHELSEA TABLE JELLY has been obtained solely upon the merits of the article, and it is held to be the greatest invention of the kind, bringing within the reach of all classes this hitherto almost unobtainable luxury. This has been fully endorsed by the unsolicited testimony of high-class British journals.

The article is put up in cardboard boxes, in quantities to make ½-pints, pints, and quarts of Jelly, and the following are some of the flavours: Lemon, Orange, Vanilla, Calves' Feet, Noyeau, Raspberry, Punch, and Madeira. It should not be confounded with the ordinary fruit Jelly, which is a totally different article, *this being a pure Calves' Feet Jelly*, superseding the use of gelatine in packets for jelly purposes—this latter, as will easily be seen, being now a thing of the past. On each box is printed a public analyst's report, also full directions for use.

The following advantages are claimed over all other Calves Feet Jellies:—
1. It is less than one-third of the price of bottled Jellies, and superior in quality.
2. It never gets mildewed or corky.
3. It never fails to set or jellify.
4. Its extreme simpleness of preparation, only requiring to be melted by the addition of hot ater, no flavouring or other matter being required.
5. It will keep good for any time until made up, when it will keep good longer than other jellies.
6. The largest quantity can be made in a few minutes.

For persons suffering from dyspepsia or any other ailment, it will also be found to be a great boon, as it can be cut and eaten in the solidified state with great satisfaction. On sea voyages and excursions of any kind it will be found invaluable.

BEWARE OF SPURIOUS IMITATIONS, and ask only for the WALTER ROBERTSON CHELSEA TABLE JELLY.

Articles of merit are often pirated by unprincipled traders.
To be had of all GROCERS, STORES, and CONFECTIONERS.

CERTIFICATE OF ANALYSIS.
Sample of CHELSEA TABLE JELLY. Received 1888.
I certify that the following are the results of the analysis of the above samples:
I have examined a sample of Chelsea Table Jelly, and find it to be a mixture of Calves' Feet Jelly and sugar; it is undoubtedly nutritious and wholesome.
It is superior to other samples that I have analysed, as it is much firmer and keeps well.
It is clear and bright, and has evidently been carefully manufactured from pure materials.
It has a pleasant flavour, and is of excellent quality.
(*Signed*) R. H. HARLAND, F.I.C., F.C.S.
Laboratory, Plough Court, 37, Lombard Street. *Public Analyst.*

Copy of Testimonial received August 26th, 1891 (unsolicited).
59, Windsor Road, Southport. *August 25th,* 1891.
GENTLEMEN,—I may inform you that I have tried other makers of jellies, but have found none to equal yours in excellence of quality. I have mentioned this fact frequently to Mr. Seymour Mead and to my friends. I am also deeply indebted to you from the fact that a little niece of mine was fed almost exclusively on your Calves' Feet Jelly for a period of three months, and who, when she refused to take other things, always took most willingly to your jellies.
Yours respectfully,
W. ROBERTSON & Co. M. T. HANSON.
This and others may be inspected at the Works, Chelsea, London.

Inventors and Sole Manufacturers (Wholesale only):
WALTER ROBERTSON & CO., CHELSEA, LONDON, S.W., ENGLAND

[Face Contents.

CONTENTS.

		PAGE.
Chap. I.—Soups		17
„ II.—Sauces		44
„ III.—Rice, Macaroni, Oatmeal		60
„ IV.—Eggs and Omelets		78
„ V.—Salads and Sandwiches		96
„ VI.—Savoury Dishes		108
„ VII.—Vegetables, Substantial		122
„ VIII.—Vegetables, Fresh		137
„ IX.—Preserved Vegetables and Fruits		152
„ X.—Jellies (Vegetarian) and Jams		158
„ XI.—Creams, Custards, and Cheesecakes		165
„ XII.—Stewed Fruits and Fruit Ices		171
„ XIII.—Cakes and Bread		177
„ XIV.—Pies and Puddings		182

E. F. LANGDALE'S
PRIZE MEDAL
Flavouring Essences and Domestic Specialities
FOR PIES, PUDDINGS, SOUPS, GRAVIES, ICES, &c.

Prepared direct from Herbs, Fruits, and Spices, gathered in their bloom and freshness.

Specially awarded Prize Medals, Great International Exhibition, London, 1851 and 1862.

(Recommended for all the Recipes in this work.)

"E. F. LANGDALE'S" *should always be insisted upon. They are Purest, Best, and Cheapest.*

Essence Lemon.	Essence Ginger.
Strong Essence Vanilla.	,, Orange.
Purified Essence Almonds.	,, Ratafia.
Essence Noyau.	,, Celery.
,, Raspberries.	,, Strawberries.

E. F. LANGDALE'S
Fruit Pudding, Blancmange, and Custard Powders
MAKE DELICIOUS PUDDINGS, CUSTARDS, & BLANCMANGE.

In 2d. and 6d. Packets. Sold everywhere.

ALMOND.	RASPBERRY.	STRAWBERRY.
LEMON.	PINE APPLE.	NECTARINE.
VANILLA.	RATAFIA.	CHOCOLATE, &c.

E. F. LANGDALE'S
Prepared Dried English Herbs, &c.

Garden Mint.	Parsley.	Lemon Thyme.	Mixed Sweet Herbs.	Tarragon.
Savoury.	Sage.	Basil.	,, Soup ,,	
	Celery Seeds.	Celery Salt.	Herbaceous Mixture.	

E. F. LANGDALE'S REFINED JAMAICA LIME JUICE AND PURE LEMON JUICE.
Distilled Tarragon and Chili Vinegar for Salads and Sauces.

Sole Agent for

J. Delcroix & Cie. Concentrated Parisian Essence,
FOR BROWNING GRAVIES, &c. (*See pages* 20, 22.)

Which should always be bought with their Name. As used by all *Chefs*.

J. DELCROIX & CIE. Pure Green Vegetable Coloured Spinach Extract. *Perfectly Harmless.*

J. DELCROIX & CIE. Brilliant Extract Cochineal for Tinting Ices, Pies, &c.

E. F. LANGDALE'S "Essence Distillery,"
72 & 73, HATTON GARDEN, LONDON, E.C. Estab. 1770.

Pamphlets, Recipes, &c., post free. All the above can be obtained of any leading Grocer. We will send name of nearest Agent on receipt of post card. [2

[Back of Contents.

INTRODUCTION.

We wish it to be distinctly understood at starting, that the present work is purely a cookery-book, written on the principles generally adopted by vegetarians; and as, until quite recently, there seemed to be in the minds of many some doubt as to the definition of vegetarianism, we will quote the following explanation from the head of the report of the London Vegetarian Society :—" The aims of the London Vegetarian Society are to advocate the total disuse of the flesh of animals (fish, flesh, and fowl) as food, and to promote a more extensive use of pulse, grains, fruits, nuts, and other products of the vegetable kingdom, thus propagating a principle tending essentially to true civilisation, to universal humaneness, and to the increase of happiness generally."

We have no intention of writing a treatise on vegetarianism, but we consider a few words of explanation necessary. Years back many persons were under the impression that by vegetarianism was meant simply an abstention from flesh-meat, but that fish was allowed. Such, however, is not the case, according to the rules of most of the Vegetarian Societies of the day. On the other hand, strictly speaking, real vegetarians would not be allowed the use of eggs and milk; but it appears that many use these, though there are a considerable number of persons who abstain. There is no doubt that the vegetable kingdom, without either milk or eggs, contains every requisite for the support of the human body. In speaking on this subject, Sir Henry Thompson observes :—" The vegetable kingdom comprehends the cereals, legumes, roots, starches, sugar, herbs, and fruits. Persons who style themselves vegetarians often consume milk, eggs, butter, and lard, which are choice foods from the animal kingdom. There are other persons, of course, who are strictly vegetarian eaters, and such alone have any right to the title of vegetarians."

In the following pages will be found ample recipes for the benefit of parties who take either view. In questions of this kind there will always be found conflicting views. We have no wish or desire to give opinions, but consider it will be more advisable, and probably render the book far more useful, if we confine ourselves as much as possible to facts.

The origin of vegetarianism is as old as the history of the world itself, and probably from time immemorial there have been sects which have practised vegetarianism, either as a religious duty, or under the belief that they would render the body more capable of performing religious duties. In the year 1098, or two years prior to the date of Henry I., there was a strictly vegetarian society formed in connection with the Christian Church, which lived entirely on herbs and roots, and the society has lasted to the present day. Again, there have been many sects who, not so strict, have allowed themselves the use of fish.

Again, there are those who adopt a vegetarian course of diet on the ground of health. Many maintain that diseases like gout and dyspepsia would disappear were vegetarian diet strictly adhered to. On the other hand, we have physicians who maintain that the great cause of indigestion is not eating enough. An American physician, some years ago, alleged he had discovered the cause, his argument being that the more work the stomach had to do the stronger it would become, on the same principle that the arm of a blacksmith is more powerful in consequence of hard work. Of one thing we are certain, and that is, there will always be rival physicians and rival sects; but the present work will simply be a guide to *those who require, from whatever cause, a light form of diet.* Perhaps the greatest benefit vegetarians can do their cause—and there are many who think very strongly on the subject—is to endeavour to take a dispassionate view. Rome was not built in a day; and if we look back at the past history of this country, during the last half-century, in regard to food, we shall see that there have been many natural changes at work. Waves of thought take place backwards and forwards, but still the tide may flow. Some fifty years ago there was, undoubtedly, a strong impression (with a large number of right-minded people) that plenty of meat, beer, and wine were good for all, even for young children. The medical profession are very apt to run in flocks, and follow some well-known leader. At the period to which we refer, numbers of anxious mothers would have regarded the advice to bring up their children as vegetarians and teetotallers as positive cruelty. This old-fashioned idea has passed away.

One great motive for adopting a course of vegetarian diet is economy; and here we feel that we stand on firm ground, without danger of offending sincere opinions, which are often wrongly called prejudices. To a great extent, the majority of the human race are virtually vegetarians from necessity. Nor do we find feebleness either of mind or body necessarily ensues. We believe there are tens of thousands of families who would give vegetarianism a trial were it not for fear. Persons are too apt to think that bodily strength depends upon the nature of the food we eat. In India we have a feeble race, living chiefly on rice. On the other hand, in China, for bodily strength, few can compare with the Coolies. For many years in Scotland the majority lived on oatmeal, while in Ireland they lived on potatoes. We do not wish to argue anything from these points, but to bring them forward for consideration. Probably, strength of body and mind, as a general rule, depends upon breed, and this argument tells two ways—it does not follow that vegetarians will be necessarily strong, and will cease to be cruel; nor does it follow that those who have been accustomed all their lives to eat meat will cease to be strong should they become vegetarians. As we have said, the great motive that induces many to give vegetarianism a trial is economy; and if persons would once get rid of the idea that they risk their health by making a trial, much would be done to advance the cause.

Another great reason for persons hesitating to make a trial is the revolution it would create in their households. Here again we are beset by difficulties, and these difficulties can only disappear gradually, after long years of patience. We believe the progress towards vegetarianism must of necessity be a very slow one. No large West End tradesman could possibly insist upon his whole establishment becoming vegetarians because he becomes one himself. We believe and hope that the present work will benefit those who are undergoing a slow but gradual change in their mode of living. This is easiest in small households, where no servants are kept at all, where the mistress is both cook and mother. It is in such households that the change is possible, and very often most desirable. In many cases trial will be made gradually. The great difficulty to contend with is prejudice, or, rather, we may say, habit. There are many housekeepers who feel that their bill of fare would instantly become extremely limited were they to adopt vegetarian ideas. There are few better dinners —especially for children—than a good basin of soup, with plenty of bread; yet, as a rule, there are few housekeepers who would know how to make vegetarian soup at all. In our present work we have given a list of sixty-four soups. At any rate, here is no lack of variety, as small housekeepers in this country are not famed for their knowledge of soup making, even with gravy-beef at their disposal.

On looking down this list it will be observed that in many cases cream—or, at any rate, milk—is recommended. We can well imagine the housekeeper exclaiming, "I don't call this economy." This is one point about which we consider a few words of explanation necessary. We will suppose a family of eight, who have been accustomed to live in the ordinary way, are going to have a vegetarian dinner by way of trial. Some soup has to be made, and one or two vegetables from the garden or the greengrocer's, as the case may be, are going to be cooked on a new method, and the housekeeper is horrified at the amount of butter she finds recommended for the sauce. People must, however, bear in mind that changes are gradual, and that often, at first starting, a degree of richness, or what they would consider extravagance, is advisable if they wish to *reconcile others* to the change. In our dinner for eight we would first ask them how much meat would they have allowed a head? At the very lowest computation, it could not have been decently done under a quarter of a pound each, even if the dish of meat took the economical form of an Irish stew; and had a joint, such as a leg of mutton, been placed upon the table, it would probably have been considerably more than double. Supposing, however, instead of the meat, we have three vegetables—say haricot beans, potatoes, and a cabbage. With the assistance of some really good butter sauce, these vegetables, eaten with bread, make an agreeable meal, which, especially in hot weather, would probably be a pleasant change. Supposing, for the sake of argument, you use half a pound of butter in making the butter sauce. This sounds, to ordinary cooks, very extravagant, even supposing butter to be only one shilling per pound. Suppose, however, this half a pound of butter is used as a means of going without a leg of mutton? That is the chief point to be borne in mind in a variety of recipes to follow. The cream, butter, and eggs are often recommended in what will appear as wholesale quantities, but, as a set-off against this, you have no butcher's bill at all. We do not maintain that this apparently unlimited use of butter, eggs, and occasionally cream, is necessary; but we believe that there are many families who will be only able to make the change by substituting "*nice*" dishes, at any rate at first starting, to make up for the loss of the meat. It is only by substituting a pleasant kind of food, that many will be induced even to attempt to change. Gradually the living will become cheaper and cheaper; but it is unwise to attempt, in a family, to do too much at once.

There are many soups we have given in which cream is recommended; for instance, artichoke soup, bean soup, cauliflower soup, and celery soup. After partaking of a well-made basin of one of these soups, followed by one or two vegetables and a fruit pie or stewed fruit, there are many persons who would voluntarily remark, "I don't seem to care for any meat." On the other hand, were the vegetables served in the old-fashioned style, but without any meat, there are many who would feel that they were undergoing a species of privation, even if they did not say so—we refer to a dish of plain-boiled potatoes and dry bread, or even the ordinary cabbage served in the usual way. Supposing, however, a nice little new cabbage is sent to table, with plenty of really good white sauce or butter sauce, over which has been sprinkled a little bright green parsley, whilst some crisp fried bread surrounds the dish—the cabbage is converted into a meal; and if we take into account the absence of the meat, we still save enormously. The advice we would give, especially to young house-keepers, is, "Persuasion is better than force." If you wish to teach a child to swim, it is far easier to entice him into shallow water on a hot summer's day than to throw him in against his will in winter time.

Another point which we consider of great importance is appearances. As far as possible, we should endeavour to make the dishes look pretty. We are appealing to a very large class throughout the country who at all cost wish to keep up appearances. It is an important class, and one on which the slow but gradual march of civilisation depends. We fear that any attempt to improve the extreme poor, who live surrounded by dirt and misery, would be hopeless, unless they still have some lingering feeling of this self-respect. For the poor woman who snatches a meal off bread-and-dripping, which she eats without a table-cloth, and then repairs to the gin-shop to wash it down, nothing can be done. This class will gradually die out as civilisation advances. This is seen, even in the present day, in America.

Fortunately, there is plenty of scope in vegetarian cooking not merely for refinement, but even elegance. Do not despise the sprinkle of chopped parsley and red specks of bread-crumbs coloured with cochineal, so often referred to throughout the following pages. Remember that the cost of these little accessories to comfort is virtually *nil*. We must remember also that one sense works upon another. We can please the palate through the eye. There is some undoubted connection between these senses. If you doubt it, suck a lemon in front of a German band and watch the result. The sight of meat causes the saliva to run from the mouths of the carnivorous animals at the Zoo. This is often noticeable in the case of a dog watching people eat, and it is an old saying, "It makes one's mouth water to look at it." In the case of endeavouring to induce a change of living in grown-up persons, such as husband or children, there is perhaps no method we can pursue so efficacious as that of making dishes look pretty. A dish of bright red tomatoes, reposing on the white bosom of a bed of macaroni, relieved here and there by a few specks of green —what a difference to a similar dish all mashed up together, and in which the macaroni showed signs of dirty smears!

We have endeavoured throughout this book to give chiefly directions about those dishes which will replace meat. For instance, the vast majority of pies and puddings will remain the same, and need no detailed treatment here. Butter supplies the place of suet or lard, and any ordinary cookery-book will be found sufficient for the purpose; but it is in dealing with soups, sauces, rice, macaroni, and vegetables, sent to table under new conditions, that we hope this book will be found most useful.

As a rule, English women cooks, especially when their title to the name depends upon their being the mistress of the house, will often find that soups and sauces are a weak point. Do not despise, in cooking, little things. Those who really understand such matters will know how vast is the difference in flavour occasioned by the addition of that pinch of thyme or teaspoonful of savoury herbs, and yet there are tens of thousands of houses, where meat is eaten every day, who never had a bottle of thyme at their disposal in their lives. As we have said, if we are going to make a great saving on meat, we can well afford a few trifles, so long as they are trifles. A sixpenny bottle of thyme will last for months; and if we give up our gravy beef, or piece of pickled pork, or twopennyworth of bones, as the case may be, surely we can afford a little indulgence of this kind.

A few words on the subject of fritters. When will English housekeepers grasp the idea of frying? They cannot get beyond a dab of grease or butter in a frying-pan. The bath of boiling oil seems to be beyond them, or at any rate a degree of civilisation that has not yet passed beyond the limit of the fried-fish shop. The oil will do over and over again, and in the end is undoubtedly cheaper than the dab of grease or butter thrown away. There are hundreds of men who, in hot weather, would positively prefer a well-cooked vegetable fritter to meat, but yet they rarely get it at home. Fruit fritters are also very economical—orange fritters, apple fritters, &c., because the batter helps to make the dish *a meal*.

Those who have practised vegetarianism for many years will probably be of opinion that we have not called sufficient attention to the subject of fruit and nuts. This is not because we do not believe in their usefulness, but because we think that those who are *changing* their mode of living will be far better enabled to do so without discomfort by making their chief alterations in diet in the directions we have pointed out. There is moreover little or no *cookery* involved in these articles.

Of the wholesomeness of fresh fruit all are agreed; and as people become more advanced vegetarians, the desire for fruit and nuts will follow in due course. In future years, as the demand increases, the supply will increase; but this is a question of time. Lookers-on often see more of the game than the players. It is not because the sudden change might not be beneficial, but because sudden changes are only likely to be effected in rare instances, that we have taken the view we have. Prejudice is strong, and it would be very difficult to persuade persons, unless they had been gradually brought to the change, to regard nuts in the light of food. To suggest a meal off Brazil nuts would to many have a tendency to put vegetarianism in a ridiculous light, and nothing kills so readily as ridicule.

In conclusion, it will be observed that from time to time we have used the expression, "if wine be allowed." There is no necessary connection between vegetarianism and teetotalism, but it would be affectation to deny the fact that they are generally connected. Of the numerous arguments brought forward by the advocates of vegetarianism, one is that, in the opinion of many who speak with authority, a vegetarian diet is best adapted to those—of whom, unfortunately, there are many—who, from time to time, have a craving for more stimulant than is beneficial to their health. Many medical men are of the opinion that large meat-eaters require alcoholic stimulant, and that they can give up the latter more easily by abstaining from the former. This is a question for medical men to decide, as it does not properly come into the province of the cook.

We have repeatedly mentioned the addition of wine and liqueurs; but when these are used for flavouring purposes it is not to be regarded in the same light as if taken alone. There is a common sense in these matters which should never be overlooked. The teetotaler who attended the Lord Mayor's dinner, and refused his glass of punch with his turtle-soup, would be consistent; but to refuse the turtle-soup itself on the ground that a little wine, probably Madeira, might have been added, would proclaim him to be a faddist. It is to be regretted that in the present day so many good causes have been injured by this ostentation of carrying ideas to an extreme. Practically, where wine is used in cookery, it is added solely for the peculiar flavour, and *the alcohol itself is evaporated*. To be consistent, the vast majority of teetotal drinks, and possibly even stewed fruit itself, would have to be refused on the same ground, viz., an almost infinitely small trace of alcohol. We think it best to explain the reason we have introduced the expression, "if wine be allowed." In each case it is used for flavouring, and flavouring purposes only. We know that with some persons a very small amount of stimulant creates a desire for more, and when this is the case the small quantity should be avoided; but in the case of the quantity being so infinitely small that it ceases to have this effect, even if not boiled away as it really is, no harm can possibly arise. Where wine is added to soups and sauces and exposed to heat, this would be the case. On the other hand, in the case of tipsy-cake, and wine added to *compote* of fruit, this would probably not be the case. A great distinction should be drawn between such cases. It will be found, however, that in every case we have mentioned the addition is altogether optional, or a substitute like lemon-juice can be used in its place.

VEGETARIAN COOKERY.

CHAPTER 1.

SOUPS.

GENERAL INSTRUCTIONS.

THERE are very few persons, unless they have made vegetarian cookery a study, who are aware what a great variety of soups can be made without the use of meat or fish. As a rule, ordinary cookery-books have the one exception of what is called *soup maigre*. In England it seems to be the impression that the goodness of the soup depends upon the amount of nourishment that can be compressed into a small space. It is, however, a great mistake to think that because we take a large amount of nourishment we are necessarily nourished. There is a limit, though what that limit is no one can say, beyond which soup becomes absolutely injurious. A quarter of a pound of Liebig's Extract of Meat dissolved in half a pint of water is obviously an over-dose of what is considered nourishment. In France, as a rule, soup is prepared on an altogether different idea. It is a light, thin broth, taken at the commencement of the meal to strengthen the stomach, in order to render it capable of receiving more substantial food to follow. Vegetarian soups are, of course, to be considered from this latter point of view.

We think these few preliminary observations necessary as we have to overcome a very strong English prejudice, which is too apt to despise everything of which the remark can be made—"Ah! but there is very little nourishment in it." Vegetarian soups, as a rule, and especially the thin ones, must be regarded as a light and pleasant flavouring which, with a small piece of white bread, enables the most obstinately delicate stomach to commence a repast that experience has found best adapted to its requirements.

The basis of all soup is stock, and in making stock we, of course, have to depend upon vegetables, fruit, or some kind of farinaceous food. To a certain extent the water in which any kind of vegetable has been boiled may be regarded as stock, especially water that has boiled roots, such as potatoes; or grains, such as rice. It will not, however, be necessary to enter into any general description as to the best method of obtaining nutriment in a liquid form from vegetables and grain, as directions will be given in each recipe, but a few words are necessary on the general subject of flavouring stock. In making ordinary soup we are very much dependent for flavour, if the soup be good, on the meat, the vegetables acting only as accessories. In making stock for vegetarian soups we are chiefly dependent for flavour on the vegetables themselves, and consequently great care must be taken that these flavourings are properly *blended*. The great difficulty in giving directions in cookery-books, and in understanding them when given, is the insuperable one of avoiding vague expressions. For instance, suppose we read, "Take two onions, one carrot, one turnip, and one head of celery,"—what does this mean? It will be found practically that these directions vary considerably according to the neighbourhood or part of the country in which we live. For instance, so much depends upon where we take our head of celery from. Suppose we bought our head of celery in Bond Street or the Central Arcade in Covent Garden Market on the one hand, or off a barrow in the Mile End Road on the other. Again, onions vary so much in size that we cannot draw any hard-and-fast line between a little pickling onion no bigger than a marble and a Spanish onion as big as a baby's head. It would be possible to be very precise and say, "Take so many ounces of celery, or so many pounds of carrot, but practically we cannot turn the kitchen into a chemist's shop. Cooks, whether told to use celery in heads or ounces, would act on guess-work just the same. What are absolutely essential are two things—common sense and experience.

Again, practically, we must avoid giving too many ingredients. Novices in the art of cooking are, of course, unable to distinguish between those vegetables that are absolutely essential and those added to give a slight extra flavour, but which make very little difference to the soup whether they are added or not. We are often directed to add a few leaves of tarragon, or chervil, or a handful of sorrel. Of course, in a large kitchen, presided over by a Francatelli, these are easily obtainable; but in ordinary private houses, and in most parts of the country, they are not only unobtainable but have never even been heard of at the greengrocer's shop.

In making soups, as a rule, the four vegetables essential are, onion, celery, carrot and turnip; and we place them in their order of merit. In making vegetarian soup it is very important that we should learn how to blend these without making any one flavour too predominant. This can only be learnt by experience. If we have too much onion the soup tastes rank; too much celery will make it bitter; too much carrot often renders the soup sweet; and the turnip overpowers every other flavour. Again, these vegetables vary so much in strength that were we to peel and weigh them the result would not be uniform, in addition to the fact that not one cook in a thousand would take the trouble to do it. Perhaps the most dangerous vegetable with which we have to deal is turnip. These vary so very much in strength that sometimes even one slice of turnip will be found too strong. In flavouring soups with these vegetables, the first care should be to see that they are thoroughly cleansed. In using celery, too much of the green part should be avoided if you wish to make first-rate soup. In using the onions, if they are old and strong, the core can be removed. In using carrot, if you are going to have any soup where vegetables will be cut up and served in the soup, you should always peel off the outside red part of the carrot and reserve it for this purpose, and only use the inside or yellow part for flavouring purposes if it is going to be thrown away or to lose its identity by being rubbed through a wire sieve with other vegetables. With regard to turnip, we can only add one word of caution—not too much. We may here mention, before leaving the subject of ingredients, that leeks and garlic are a substitute for onion, and can also be used in conjunction with it.

As a rule, in vegetarian cookery clear soups are rare, and, of course, from an economical point of view, they are not to be compared with thick soups. Some persons, in making stock, recommend what is termed bran tea. Half a pint of bran is boiled in about three pints of water, and a certain amount of nutriment can be extracted from the bran, which also imparts colour.

For the purpose of colouring clear soups, however, there is nothing in the world to compare with what French cooks call *caramel*. Caramel is really burnt sugar. There is a considerable art in preparing it, as it is necessary that it should impart colour, and colour *only*. When prepared in the rough-and-ready manner of burning sugar in a spoon, as is too often practised in English kitchens, this desideratum is never attained, as you are bound to impart sweetness in addition to a burnt flavour. The simplest and by far the most economical method of using caramel is to buy it ready-made. It is sold by all grocers under the name of Parisian Essence. A small bottle, costing about eightpence, will last a year, and saves an infinite loss of time, trouble, and temper.

By far the most economical soups are the thick, where all the ingredients can be rubbed through a wire sieve. Thick soups can be divided into two classes—ordinary brown soup, and white soup. The ordinary brown is the most economical, as in white soups milk is essential, and if the soup is wished to be very good it is necessary to add a little cream.

Soups owe their thickness to two processes. We can thicken the soup by adding flour of various kinds, such as ordinary flour, corn-flour, &c., and soup can also be thickened by having some of the ingredients of which it is composed rubbed through a sieve. This class of soups may be called Purées. For instance, Palestine soup is really a purée of Jerusalem artichokes; ordinary pea soup is a purée of split peas. In making our ordinary vegetarian soups of all kinds, as a rule, all the ingredients should be rubbed through a sieve. The economy of this is obvious on the face of it. In the case of thickening soup by means of some kinds of flour, for richness and flavour there is nothing to equal ordinary flour that has been cooked. This is what Frenchmen call roux.

As white and brown roux are the very backbone of vegetarian cookery a few words of explanation may not be out of place. On referring to the recipe for making white and brown roux, it will be seen that it is simply flour cooked by means of frying it in butter. In white roux each grain of flour is cooked till it is done. In brown roux each grain of flour is cooked till it is done brown. We cannot exaggerate the importance of getting cooks to see the enormous difference between thickening soups or gravy with white or brown roux and simply thickening them with plain butter and flour. The taste of the soup in the two cases is altogether different. The difference is this. Suppose you have just been making some pastry—some good, rich, puff paste—you have got two pies, and, as you probably know, this pastry is simply butter and flour. Place one pie in the oven and bake it till it is a nice rich brown. Now taste the pie-crust. It is probably delicious. Now taste the piece of the pie that has not been baked at all. It is nauseous. The difference is—one is butter and flour that has been cooked, the other is butter and flour that has not been cooked.

One word of warning in conclusion. Cooks should always remember the good old saying—that it is quite possible to have too much of a good thing. They should be particularly warned to bear this in mind in adding herbs, such as ordinary mixed flavouring herbs, or, as they are sometimes called, savoury herbs, and thyme. This is also very important if wine is added to soup, though, as a rule, vegetarians rarely use wine in cooking; but the same principle applies to the substitute for wine—viz., lemon juice. It is equally important to bear this in mind in using white and brown roux. If we make the soup too thick we spoil it, and it is necessary to add water to bring it to its proper consistency, which, of course, diminishes the flavour. The proper consistency of any soup thickened with roux should be that of ordinary cream. Beyond this point the cooked flour will overpower almost every other flavour, and the great beauty of vegetarian cookery is its simplicity. It appeals to a taste that is refined and natural, and not to one that has been depraved.

Stock.—Strictly speaking, in vegetarian cookery, stock is the goodness and flavouring that can be extracted from vegetables, the chief ones being onion, celery, carrot, and turnip. In order to make stock, take these vegetables, cut them up into small pieces, after having thoroughly cleansed them, place them in a saucepan with sufficient water to cover them, and let them boil gently for several hours. The liquor, when strained off, may be called stock. It can be flavoured with a small quantity of savoury herbs, pepper, and salt, as well as a little mushroom ketchup. It can be coloured with a few drops of Parisian essence, or burnt sugar. Its consistency can be improved by the addition of a small quantity of corn-flour. Sufficient corn-flour must be added not to make it thick but like very thin gum. In a broader sense, the water in which rice, lentils, beans and potatoes have been boiled may be called stock. Again, the water in which macaroni, vermicelli, sparghetti, and all kinds of Italian paste has been boiled, may be called stock. The use of liquors of this kind must be left to the common sense of the cook, as, of course, it would only be obtainable when these materials are required for use.

Brown and White Thickening, or Roux.—It is of great importance for vegetarians always to have on hand a fairly good stock of white and brown roux, as it is a great saving both of time and money. As roux will keep good for weeks, and even months, there is no fear of waste in making a quantity at a time. Take a pound of flour, with a spoonful or two over; see that it is thoroughly dry, and then sift it. Next take a pound of butter and squeeze it in a cloth so as as much as possible to extract all the moisture from it. Next take a stew-pan—an enamelled one is best—and melt the butter till it runs to oil. It will now be found that, although the bulk of the butter looks like oil, a certain amount of froth will rise to the top. This must be carefully skimmed off. Continue to expose the butter to a gentle heat till the scum ceases to rise. Now pour off the oiled butter very gently into a basin till you come to some dregs. These should be thrown away, or, at any rate, not used in making the roux. Now mix the pound of dried and sifted flour with the oiled butter, which is what the French cooks call clarified butter. Place it back in the stew-pan, put the stew-pan over a tolerably good fire, but not too fierce, as there is a danger of its burning. With a wooden spoon keep stirring this mixture, and keep scraping the bottom of the stew-pan, first in one place and then in another, being specially careful of the edges, to prevent its burning. Gradually the mixture will begin to turn colour. As soon as this turn of colour is perceptible take out half and put it in a basin. This is the white roux, viz., flour cooked in butter but not discoloured beyond a very trifling amount. Keep the stew-pan on the fire, and go on stirring the remainder, which will get gradually darker and darker in colour. As soon as the colour is that of light chocolate remove the stew-pan from the fire altogether, but still continue scraping and stirring for a few minutes longer, as the enamel retains the heat to such an extent that it will sometimes burn after it has been removed from the fire. It is important not to have the mixture too dark, and it will be found by experience that it gets darker after the stew-pan has been removed from the fire. When we say light chocolate we refer to the colour of a cake of chocolate that has been broken. The inside is the colour, not the outside. It is advisable sometimes to have by you ready a large slice of onion, and if you think it is dark enough you can throw this in and immediately by this means slacken the heat. Pour the brown roux into a separate basin, and put them by for use.

In the houses of most vegetarians more white roux will be used than brown, consequently more than half should be removed if this is the case when the roux first commences to turn colour. When the brown roux gets cold it has all the appearance of chocolate, and when you use it it is best to scrape off the quantity you require with a spoon, and not add it to soups or sauces in one lump.

Almond Soup.—Take half a pound of sweet almonds and blanch them, *i.e.*, throw them into boiling water till the outside skin can be rubbed off easily with the finger. Then immediately throw the white almonds into cold water, otherwise they will quickly lose their white colour like potatoes that have been peeled. Next, slice up an onion and half a small head of celery, and let these simmer gently in a quart of milk. In the meantime pound the almonds with four hard-boiled yolks of egg, strain off the milk and add the pounded almonds and egg to the milk gradually, and let it boil over the fire. Add sufficient white roux till the soup becomes of the consistency of cream. Serve some fried or toasted bread with the soup. It is a great improvement to add half a pint of cream, but this makes the soup much more expensive. The soup can be flavoured with a little white pepper.

N.B.—The onion and celery that was strained off can be used again for flavouring purposes.

Apple Soup.—This is a German recipe. Take half a dozen good-sized apples, peel them and remove the core, and boil them in a quart of water with two tablespoonfuls of bread-crumbs; add the juice of a lemon, and flavour it with rather less than a quarter of an ounce of powdered cinnamon; sweeten the soup with lump sugar, previously having rubbed six lumps on the outside of the lemon.

Artichoke Soup.—Take a dozen large Jerusalem artichokes about as big as the fist, or more to make up a similar quantity. Peel them, and, like potatoes, throw them into cold water in order to prevent them turning colour. Boil them in as little water as possible, as they contain a good deal of water themselves, till they are tender and become a pulp, taking care that they do not burn, and therefore it is best to rub the saucepan at the bottom with a piece of butter. Now rub them through a wire sieve and add them to a pint of milk in which a couple of bay-leaves have been boiled. Add also two lumps of sugar and a little white pepper and salt. Serve the soup with fried or toasted bread. This soup can be made much richer by the addition of either a quarter of a pint of cream or a couple of yolks of eggs. If yolks of eggs are added, beat up the yolks separately and add the soup gradually, very hot, but not quite boiling, otherwise the yolks will curdle.

Asparagus Soup.—Take a good-sized bundle (about fifty large heads) of asparagus, and after a thorough cleansing throw them into a saucepan of boiling water that has been salted. When the tops become tender, drain off the asparagus and throw it into cold water, as by this means we retain the bright green colour; when cold cut off all the best part of the green into little pieces, about half an inch long, then put the remainder of the asparagus—the stalk part—into a saucepan, with a few green onions and a few sprigs of parsley, with about a quart of stock or water; add a teaspoonful of pounded sugar and a very little grated nutmeg. Let this boil till the stalks become quite tender, then rub the whole through a wire sieve and thicken the soup with a little white roux, and colour it a bright green with some spinach extract. Now add the little pieces cut up, and let the whole simmer gently, and serve fried or toasted bread with the soup.

N.B.—**Spinach Extract.**—It is very important in making all green vegetable soups that they should be of a green colour, such as the one above mentioned—green-pea soup, &c., and that we get a *good* colour, and this is only to be obtained by means of spinach extract. Spinach extract can be made at home, but it will be found to be far more economical to have a small bottle of green vegetable colouring always in the house. These bottles can be obtained from all grocers at the cost of about tenpence or one shilling each. Such a very small quantity goes such a long way that one bottle would probably last a family of six persons twelve months. As we have said, it can be made at home, but the process, though not difficult, is troublesome. It is made as follows :—A quantity of spinach has, after being thoroughly washed, to be pounded in a mortar until it becomes a pulp. This pulp is then placed in a very strong, coarse cloth, and the cloth is twisted till the juice of the spinach is squeezed out through the cloth. The amount of force required is very considerable and is almost beyond the power of ordinary women cooks. This juice must now be placed in a small enamelled saucepan, and must be heated till it becomes thick and pulpy, when it can be put by for use. It will probably be found cheaper to buy spinach extract than to make it, as manual labour cannot compete with machinery.

Barley Soup.—Take two tablespoonfuls of pearl barley and wash it in several waters till the water ceases to be discoloured. Put this in a saucepan with about two quarts of water, two onions sliced up, a few potatoes sliced very thin, and about a saltspoonful of thyme. Let the whole boil gently for four or five hours, till the barley is quite soft and eatable. Thicken the soup very slightly with a little white roux, season it with pepper and salt. Before serving the soup, add a tablespoonful of chopped blanched parsley.

B *

N.B.—When chopped parsley is added to any soup or sauce, such as parsley and butter, it is very important that the parsley be blanched. To blanch parsley means to throw it for a few seconds into boiling water. By this means a dull green becomes a bright green. The best method to blanch parsley is to place it in a strainer and dip the strainer for a few seconds in a saucepan of boiling water. By comparing the colour of the parsley that has been so treated with some that has not been blanched, cooks will at once see the importance of the operation so far as appearances are concerned.

Beetroot Soup.—This soup is better adapted to the German palate than the English, as it contains both vinegar and sugar, which are very characteristic of German cookery. Take two large beetroots and two good-sized onions, and after peeling the beetroots boil them and mince them finely, adding them, of course, to the water in which they were boiled, or still better, they can be boiled in some sort of stock. Add a very small quantity of corn-flour, to give a slight consistency to the soup, as well as a little pinch of thyme. Next add two tablespoonfuls of vinegar—more or less according to taste—a spoonful of brown sugar, and a little pepper and salt.

Bean Soup, or Purée of Red Haricot Beans.—Put a quart of red haricot beans into soak overnight, and put a little piece of soda in the water to soften it. The next morning put the beans on to boil in three quarts of water, with some carrot, celery and onion, or the beans can be boiled in some stock made from these vegetables. After the beans are tender, pound them in a mortar, and then rub the whole through a wire sieve, after first removing the carrot, celery and onion. Add a teaspoonful of pounded sugar and about two ounces of butter. Fried or toasted bread should be served with the soup. If the soup is liked thin, of course more water can be added.

Bean Soup, or Purée of White Haricot Beans.—Proceed exactly as in the above recipe, only substituting white haricot beans for red. It is a great improvement to add a little boiling cream, but of course this makes the soup much more expensive. Some cooks add a spoonful of blanched, chopped parsley to this purée, and Frenchmen generally flavour this soup with garlic.

Bean Soup, Green.—Boil a quart of ordinary broad-beans in some stock or water with an onion, carrot and celery. Remove the skins when the beans are tender and rub the beans through a wire sieve. Colour the soup with a little spinach extract— (vegetable colouring, sold in bottles)—add a little piece of butter, a little powdered sugar, pepper and salt. The amount of stock or water must depend upon whether it is wished to have the purée thick or thin. Some purées are made as thick as bread sauce, while some persons prefer them much thinner. This is purely a matter of taste.

Bean Soup from French Beans.—This is an admirable method of using up French beans or scarlet runners when they get too old to be boiled as a vegetable in the ordinary way. Take any quantity of French beans and boil them in some stock or water with an onion, carrot, or celery for about an hour, taking care, at starting, to throw them into boiling water in order to preserve their colour. It is also a saving of trouble to chop the beans slightly at starting, *i.e.*, take a bunch of beans in the left hand and cut them into pieces, say an eighth of an inch in thickness. Boil them till they are tender, and then rub the whole through a wire sieve. Add a little butter, pepper and salt, and colour the soup with spinach extract—(vegetable colouring, sold in bottles). Serve toasted or fried bread with the purée, which should be rather thick.

Cabbage Soup.—Take a white cabbage and slice it up, and throw it into some stock or water, with some leeks and slices of turnip. Boil the whole till the vegetables are tender, flavour with pepper and salt. This is sometimes called Cornish broth, though in Cornwall a piece of meat or bones are generally boiled with the vegetables. As no meat, of course, is used, too much water must not be added, but only sufficient liquor must be served to make the vegetables thoroughly moist. Perhaps the consistency can best be described by saying that there should be equal quantities of vegetables and fluid.

Carrot Soup.—If you wish this soup to be of a good colour, you must only use the outside, or red part, of the carrot, in which case a dozen large carrots will be required. If economy is practised, half this quantity will be sufficient. Take, say, half a dozen carrots, a small head of celery, and one onion, and throw them into boiling water for a few minutes in order to preserve the colour. Then drain them off and place them in a saucepan, with a couple of ounces of butter to prevent them sticking and burning, and place the saucepan on a very slack fire and let them stew so that the steam can escape, but take care they don't burn or get brown. Now add a quart or two quarts of stock or water and boil them till they are tender. Then rub the whole through a wire sieve, add a little butter, pounded sugar, pepper, and salt. The amount of liquid added must entirely depend upon the size of the carrots. It is better to add too little than too much, but the consistency of the soup should be like ordinary pea soup; it does not do to have the soup watery. If only the outside parts of carrots are used, and this red part is thrown, at starting, into boiling water to preserve its colour, this soup, when made thick, has a very bright and handsome appearance, and is suitable for occasions when a little extra hospitality is exercised. The inside part of the carrot, if not used for making the soup, need not be wasted, but can be used for making stock, or served in a dish of mixed vegetables on some other occasion.

Cauliflower Soup.—Take three or four small cauliflowers, or two large ones, soak them in salt and water, and boil them in some water till they are nearly tender. Take them out and break the cauliflower so that you get two or three dozen little pieces out of the heart of the cauliflower, somewhat resembling miniature bouquets. Put the rest of the cauliflower back into the water in which it was boiled, with the exception of the green part of the leaves, with an onion and some of the white part of a head of celery. Let all boil till the water has nearly boiled away. Now rub all this through a wire sieve, onions, celery, cauliflower, and all; add to it sufficient boiling milk to make the whole of the consistency of pea soup. Add a little butter, pepper, and salt; throw in those little pieces of cauliflower that had been reserved a minute or two before serving the soup. It is an improvement to boil two or three bay-leaves with the milk, and also a very great improvement indeed to add a little boiling cream. Fried or toasted bread should be served with the soup.

Celery Soup.—Take half a dozen heads of celery, or a smaller quantity if the heads of celery are very large; throw away all the green part and cut up the celery into small pieces, with one onion sliced, and place them in a frying-pan, or, better still, in an enamelled stew-pan, and stew them in a little butter, taking great care that the celery does not turn colour. Now add sufficient water or stock, and let it all boil till the celery becomes quite tender. Let it boil till it becomes a pulp, and then rub the whole through a wire sieve. Next boil separately from one to two quarts of milk according to the quantity of celery pulp, and boil a couple of bay-leaves in the milk. As soon as the milk boils add it to the celery pulp, flavour the soup with pepper and salt; serve fried or toasted bread with the soup. It is needless to say that all these white soups are greatly improved both in appearance and flavour by the addition of a little cream.

Cheese Soup.—Light-coloured and dry cheese is necessary for this somewhat peculiar soup, but the best cheese of all is, undoubtedly, Gruyère. Grate half a pound of cheese and spread a layer of this at the bottom of the soup-tureen. Cover this layer of cheese with some very thin slices of stale crumb of bread. Then put another layer of cheese and another layer of bread till all the cheese is used up. Next take about two tablespoonfuls of brown roux, melt this in a small saucepan, and add two tablespoonfuls of chopped onion. Let the onion cook in the melted roux over the fire, and then add a quart of water, and stir it all up till it boils, adding pepper and salt and a few drops of Parisian essence (burnt sugar) to give it a dark brown colour. Now pour the boiling soup over the contents of the soup-tureen, and let it stand a few minutes so that the bread has time to soak, and serve.

Cherry Soup.—Like most soups that are either sweet or sour, this is a German recipe. Put a piece of butter, the size of a large egg, into a saucepan. Let it melt, then mix it with a tablespoonful of flour, and stir smoothly until it is lightly browned. Add gradually two pints of water, a pound of black cherries, picked and washed, and a few cloves. Let these boil until the fruit is quite tender, then press the whole through a sieve. After straining, add a little port, if wine is allowed—but the soup will be very nice without this addition—half a teaspoonful of the kernels, blanched and bruised, a tablespoonful of sugar, and a few whole cherries. Let the soup boil again until the cherries are tender, and pour all into a tureen over toasted sippets, sponge-cakes, or macaroons.

Chestnut Soup, or Purée of Chestnuts.—Take four dozen chestnuts and peel them. This will be a very long process if we attempt to take off the skins while they are raw; but in order to save time and trouble, place the chestnuts in a stewpan with a couple of ounces of butter. Place them on a slack fire and occasionally give them a stir. Heat them gradually till the husks come off without any difficulty. Having removed all the husks, add sufficient stock or water to the chestnuts, and let them boil gently till they are tender. Then pound them in a mortar and rub them through a wire sieve. Add a very little brown roux, if the soup is to be brown, and a few drops of Parisian essence (burnt sugar), or a little white roux and a little cream if the soup is to be white. Add also a little pepper and salt, sufficient butter to make the purée taste soft, and a little powdered sugar. Fried and toasted bread should be served with the soup.

Cottage Soup.—Fry two onions, a carrot and a turnip, and a small head of celery cut up into small pieces, in a frying-pan, with a little butter, till they are lightly browned. Then put them in a saucepan, with about two quarts of water and a tablespoonful of mixed savoury herbs. Let this boil till the vegetables are quite tender, and then thicken the soup with two ounces of oatmeal or prepared barley. This must be mixed with cold water and made quite smooth before it is added to the soup. Wash a quarter of a pound of rice, and boil this in the soup, and when the rice is quite tender the soup can be served. Some persons add a little sugar, and dried powdered mint can be handed round with the soup, like pea soup.

Clear Soup.—Make a very strong stock by cutting up onion, celery, carrot, and a little turnip, and boiling them in some water. They should boil for two or three hours. Add also a teaspoonful of mixed savoury herbs to every quart, and colour the stock with a few drops of Parisian essence. Strain it off, and, if it is not bright, clear it with some white of egg in the ordinary way. Take only sufficient corn-flour to make the soup less thin or watery, but do not make it thick. A tablespoonful of mushroom ketchup can be added to every quart.

Cocoanut Soup.—Break open a good-sized cocoanut and grate sufficient of the white part till it weighs half a pound. Boil this in some stock, and after it has boiled for about an hour strain it off. Only a small quantity of stock must be used, and the cocoanut should be pressed and squeezed, so as to extract all the goodness. Add a little pepper and salt, and about half a grated nutmeg. Next boil separately three pints of milk, and add this to the strained soup. Thicken the soup with some ground rice, and serve. Of course, a little cream would be a great improvement. Serve with toasted or fried bread.

Endive Soup, or Purée.—Take half a dozen endives that are white in the centre, and wash them very thoroughly in salt and water, as they are apt to contain insects. Next throw them into boiling water, and let them boil for a quarter of an hour. Then take them out and throw them into cold water. Next take them out of the cold water and squeeze them in a cloth so as to extract all the moisture. Then cut off the root of each endive, chop up all the white leaves, and place them in a stew-pan with about two ounces of butter. Add half a grated nutmeg, a brimming teaspoonful of powdered white sugar, and a little pepper and salt. Stir them over the fire with a wooden spoon, and take care they don't burn or turn colour. Next add sufficient milk to moisten them, and let them simmer gently till they are tender ; then rub the whole through a wire sieve, add a little piece of butter, and serve with fried or toasted bread.

Fruit Soup.—Fruit soup can be made from rhubarb, vegetable marrow, cucumber, gourd, or pumpkin. They may be all mixed with a little cream, milk, or butter, and form a nice dish that is both healthful and delicate.

Green Pea Soup.—(*See* PEA.)

Green Pea Soup, Dried.—(*See* PEA.)

Hare Soup (Imitation).—Take one large carrot, a small head of celery, one good-sized onion, and half a small turnip, and boil these in a quart of water till they are tender. Rub the whole through a wire sieve, and thicken the soup with some brown roux till it is as thick as good cream. Next add a brimming saltspoonful of aromatic flavouring herbs. These herbs are sold in bottles by all grocers under the name of Herbaceous Mixture. Flavour the soup with cayenne pepper, a glass of port wine (port wine dregs will do), dissolve in it a small dessertspoonful of red-currant jelly, and add the juice of half a lemon.

N.B.—Aromatic flavouring herbs are exceedingly useful in cooking. It is cheaper to buy them ready made, under the name of Herbaceous Mixture. They can, however, be made at home as follows :—Take two ounces of white peppercorns, two ounces of cloves, one ounce of marjoram, one ounce of sweet basil and one ounce of lemon-thyme, one ounce of powdered nutmeg, one ounce of powdered mace, and half an ounce of dried bay-leaves. The herbs must be wrapped up in paper (one or two little paper bags, one inside the other, is best), and dried very slowly in the oven till they are brittle. They must then be pounded in a mortar, and mixed with the spices, and the whole sifted through a fine hair-sieve and put by in a stoppered bottle for use.

Hotch-potch.—Cut up some celery, onion, carrot, turnip, and leeks into small pieces and fry them for a few minutes in about two ounces of butter in a frying-pan, very gently, taking care that they do not in the least degree turn colour. Previous to this, wash and boil about a quarter of a pound of pearl barley for four or five hours. When the barley is tender, or nearly tender, add the contents of the frying-pan. Let it all boil till the vegetables are tender, and about half an hour before the soup is sent to table throw in, while the soup is boiling, half a pint of fresh green peas—those known as marrowfats are best,—and about five minutes before sending the soup to table throw in a spoonful (in the proportion of a dessertspoonful to every quart) of chopped, blanched parsley— *i.e.*, parsley that has been thrown into boiling water before it is chopped. Colour the soup green with a little spinach extract (vegetable colouring sold in bottles by all grocers). The thinness of the soup can be removed by the addition of a small quantity of white roux.

Jardinière Soup.—Cut up into thin strips some carrot, turnip and celery, add a dozen or more small button onions, similar to those used for pickling, and also a few hearts of lettuces cut up fine, as well as a few fresh tarragon leaves cut into strips as thin as small string. Simmer these gently in some clear soup (*see* CLEAR SOUP) till tender; add a lump of sugar, and serve.

N.B.—The tarragon should not be thrown in till the last minute.

Julienne Soup.—This soup is exactly similar to the previous one, the only exception being that all the vegetables are first stewed very gently, till they are tender, in a little butter. Care should be taken that the vegetables do not turn colour.

Leek Soup.— Take half a dozen or more fine large leeks, and after trimming off the green part, throw them into boiling water for five minutes, then drain them off and dry them. Cut them into pieces about half an inch long, and stew them gently in a little butter till they are tender. Add three pints of milk, and let two bay-leaves boil in the milk, flavour with pepper and salt, and add a suspicion of grated nutmeg. Thicken the soup with a little white roux and take the crust of a French roll. Cut this up into small pieces or rings. The rings can be made by simply scooping out the crumb, and cutting the roll across. When the leeks have boiled in the milk till they are quite tender, pour the soup over the crusts placed at the bottom of the soup-tureen. Some cooks add blanched parsley. Of course, cream would be a great improvement.

Lentil Soup.—Take a breakfastcupful of green lentils and put them to soak in cold water overnight. In the morning throw away any floating on the top. Drain the lentils and put them in a stew-pan or saucepan with some stock or water, and add two onions, two carrots, a turnip, a bunch of parsley, a small teaspoonful of savoury herbs and a small head of celery. If you have no celery add half a teaspoonful of bruised celery seed. You can also add a crust of stale bread. Let the whole boil, and it will be found that occasionally a dark film will rise to the surface. This must be skimmed off. The soup must boil for about four hours, or at any rate till the lentils are thoroughly soft. Then strain the soup through a wire sieve, and rub the whole of the contents through the wire sieve with the soup. This requires both time and patience. After the whole has been rubbed through the sieve the soup must be boiled up, and if made from green lentils it can be coloured green with some spinach extract—(vegetable colouring, sold in bottles). If made from Egyptian (red) lentils, the soup can be coloured with a few drops of Parisian essence (burnt sugar). In warming up this soup, after the lentils have been rubbed through a sieve, it should be borne in mind that the lentil powder has a tendency to settle, and consequently the saucepan must be constantly stirred to prevent it burning. In serving the soup at table, the contents of the soup-tureen should be stirred with the soup-ladle before each help.

Lentil Purée à la Soubise.—This is really lentil soup, made as above, rather thick, to which has been added a purée of onions, made as follows :—Slice up, say four large onions, and fry them brown in a little butter, then boil them in some of the broth of the soup till they are tender. Rub them through a wire sieve and add them to the soup.

Macaroni Soup (clear).—Take some macaroni and break it up into pieces about two inches long. Boil them till they are tender in some salted water, drain them off and add them to some clear soup. (*See* CLEAR SOUP.)

Macaroni Soup (thick).—Take an onion, carrot, a small head of celery and a very small quantity of turnip; cut them up and boil them in a very small quantity of water for about an hour. Then rub the whole through a wire sieve, add a quart or more of boiling milk, throw in the macaroni, after breaking it up into pieces two inches long, and let the macaroni simmer in this till it is perfectly tender. The soup should be thickened with a very little white roux, a bay-leaf can be boiled in the soup; a small quantity of cream is a great improvement. Fried or toasted bread should be served with it.

Milk Soup.—Milk soup, as it is sometimes called in Germany, very much resembles English custard. It is made by putting a quart of milk on the fire and thickening it with two yolks of eggs and a little flour, and sweetening it with sugar. The soup is flavoured with either vanilla, lemon, laurel leaves, pounded almonds, cinnamon, chocolate, &c. As a soup, however, it is not suited to the English palate.

Mock Turtle, Imitation.—Take an onion, carrot, small head of celery, and some turnip, and boil them till they are tender in some stock. The water in which some rice has been boiled is very well suited for the purpose. Add also to every quart a brimming tablespoonful of mixed savoury herbs. Rub the whole through a wire sieve, thicken it with brown roux till it is as thick as cream; add a few drops of Parisian essence—(sold in bottles by all grocers)—to give it a dark colour. Add a wineglassful of sherry or Madeira, or, if the use of wine be objected to, the juice of a hard lemon. Flavour the soup with a little cayenne pepper, and serve some egg forcemeat balls in it, about the size of small marbles.

Mulligatawny Soup.—Take four large onions, cut them up and fry them brown, with a little butter, in a frying-pan, with a carrot cut up into small pieces; add to this a quart of stock or water, and boil till the vegetables and onions are tender; then rub the whole through a wire sieve and add a brimming teaspoonful of Captain White's Curry Paste and a dessertspoonful of curry powder, previously mixed smooth in a little cold water; thicken the soup with a little brown roux. Some persons would consider this soup too hot; if so, less curry powder can be used or more water added. If you have no curry paste, cut up a sour apple and add it to the vegetables in the frying-pan. If you have no sour apples, a few green gooseberries are a very good substitute. Boiled rice should be served on a separate dish with this soup, and should not be boiled in the soup at starting.

Onion Soup.—Cut up half a dozen onions and throw them for a few minutes into boiling water. This takes off the rankness. Drain off the onions, and chop them up and boil them till they are tender in some milk that has been seasoned with pepper and salt and a pinch of savoury herbs. Take a small quantity of celery, carrot and turnip, or carrot and turnip and a little bruised celery seed, and boil till they are tender in a very little water; rub through a wire sieve, and add the pulp to the soup. The soup can be thickened with white roux, ground rice, or one or two eggs beaten up. The soup must be added to the eggs gradually or they will curdle.

Onion Soup, Brown.—Take an onion, carrot, celery, and turnip, and let them boil till quite tender in some water or stock. In the meantime slice up half a dozen large onions and fry them brown in a little butter, in a frying-pan, taking care that the onions are browned and not burnt black; add the contents of the frying-pan to the vegetables and stock, and after it has boiled some time, till the onions are tender, rub the whole through a wire sieve, thicken with a little brown roux, adding, of course, pepper and salt to taste.

Ox-tail Soup, Imitation.—Slice off the outside red part of two or three large carrots, and cut them up into small dice not bigger than a quarter of an inch square. Cut up also into similar size a young turnip, and the white, hard part of a head of celery. Fry these very gently in a little butter, taking care that the vegetables do not turn colour. Make some soup exactly in every respect similar to that described in Imitation Mock Turtle. Throw in these fried vegetables, and let the soup simmer gently by the side of the fire, in order for it to throw up its butter, which should be skimmed off. In flavouring the soup, add only half the quantity of wine or lemon juice that you would use were you making Mock Turtle.

Palestine Soup.—(*See* ARTICHOKE SOUP.)

Parsnip Soup.—Prepare half a dozen parsnips, and boil them with an onion and half a head of celery in some stock till they are quite tender. Then rub the whole through a wire sieve, boil it up again, and serve. Sufficient parsnips must be boiled to make the soup as thick as pea soup, so the quantity of stock must be regulated accordingly. This soup is generally rather sweet, owing to the parsnips, and an extra quantity of salt must be added in consequence, as well as pepper. In Belgium and Germany this sweetness is corrected by the addition of vinegar. This, of course, is a matter of taste.

Pear Soup.—Pare, core, and slice six or eight large pears. Put them into a stew-pan with a penny roll cut into thin slices, half a dozen cloves, and three pints of water. Let them simmer until they are quite tender, then pass them through a coarse sieve, and return the purée to the saucepan, with two ounces of sugar, the strained juice of a fresh lemon, and half a tumblerful of light wine. Let the soup boil five or ten minutes, when it will be ready for serving. Send some sponge-cake to table with this dish.

Pea Soup, from Split Dried Peas.—Take a pint of split peas and put them in soak overnight in some cold water, and throw away those that float, as this shows that there is a hole in them which would be mildewy. Take two onions, a carrot, a small head of celery, and boil them with the peas in from three pints to two quarts of water till they are tender. This will be from four to five hours. When the peas are old and stale even longer time should be allowed. Then rub the whole through a wire sieve, put the soup back into the saucepan, and stir it while you make it hot or it will burn. In ordinary cookery, pea soup is invariably made from some kind of greasy stock, more especially the water in which pickled pork has been boiled. In the present instance we have no kind of fat to counteract the natural dryness of the pea-flour. We must therefore add, before sending to table, two or three ounces of butter. It will be found best to dissolve the butter in the saucepan before adding the soup to be warmed up, as it is then much less likely to stick to the bottom of the saucepan and burn. Fried or toasted bread should be served with the soup separately, as well as dried and powdered mint. The general mistake people make is, they do not have sufficient mint.

Pea Soup, from Dried Green Peas.—Proceed as in the above recipe in every respect, substituting dried green peas for ordinary yellow split peas. Colour the soup green by adding a large handful of spinach before it is rubbed through the wire sieve, or add a small quantity of spinach extract (vegetable colouring sold by grocers in bottles); dried mint and fried or toasted bread should be served with the soup, as with the other.

Pea Soup, Green (Fresh).—Take half a peck of young peas, shell them, and throw the peas into cold water. Put all the shells into a quart or more of stock or water. Put in also a handful of spinach if possible, a few sprigs of parsley, a dozen fresh mint-leaves and half a dozen small, fresh, green onions. Boil these for an hour, or rather more, and then rub the whole through a wire sieve. You cannot rub all the shells through; but you will be able to rub a great part through, that which is left in the sieve being only strings. Now put on the soup to boil again, and as soon as it boils throw in the peas; as soon as these are tender—about twenty minutes—the soup is finished and can be sent to table. If the soup is thin, a little white roux can be added to thicken it; if of a bad colour, or if you could not get any spinach, add some spinach extract (vegetable colouring, sold by all grocers), only take care not to add too much, and make the soup look like green paint.

Potato Soup.—Potato soup is a very good method of using up the remains of cold boiled potatoes. Slice up a large onion and fry it, without letting it turn colour, with a little butter. Add a little water or stock to the frying-pan, and let the onion boil till it is tender. Boil a quart or more of milk separately with a couple of bay-leaves; rub the onion with the cold potatoes through a wire sieve and add it to the milk. You can moisten the potatoes in the sieve with the milk. When you have rubbed enough to make the soup thick enough, let it boil up and add to every quart a saltspoonful of thyme and a brimming teaspoonful of chopped blanched parsley. This soup should be rather thicker than most thick soups.

When new potatoes first come into season, and especially when you have new potatoes from your own garden, it will often be found that mixed with the ordinary ones there are many potatoes no bigger than a toy marble, and which are too small to be boiled and sent to table as an ordinary dish of new potatoes. Reserve all these little dwarf potatoes, wash them, and throw them for five or ten minutes into boiling water, drain them off and throw them into the potato soup whole. Of course they must boil in the soup till they are tender. A little cream is a great improvement to the soup, and dried mint can be served with it, but is not absolutely necessary.

Pumpkin Soup.—Take half or a quarter of a moderate-sized pumpkin, pare it, remove the seeds, and cut the pumpkin into thin slices. Put these into a stew-pan, with as much water or milk as will cover them, and boil gently until they are reduced to a pulp. Rub this through a fine sieve, mix with it a little salt, and a piece of butter the size of an egg, and stir it over the fire until it boils. Thin it with some boiling milk which has been sweetened and flavoured with lemon-rind, cinnamon, or orange-flower water. It should be of the consistency of thick cream. Put toasted bread, cut into the size of dice, at the bottom of the soup-tureen. Moisten the bread-dice with a small quantity of the liquor, let them soak a little while, then pour the rest of the soup over them, and serve very hot. Or whisk two fresh eggs thoroughly in the tureen, and pour the soup in over them at the last moment. The liquor ought to have ceased from boiling for a minute or two before it is poured over the eggs.

Rhubarb Soup.—This is a sweet soup, and is simply juice from stewed rhubarb sweetened and flavoured with lemon-peel and added either to cream or beaten-up yolks of eggs and a little white wine. It is rarely met with in this country.

Rice Soup.—Take a quarter of a pound of rice, and wash it in several waters till the water ceases to be discoloured. Take an onion, the white part of a head of celery, and a turnip, and cut them up and fry them in a little butter. Add a quart of stock, or water, and boil these vegetables until they are tender, and then rub them through a wire sieve. Boil the rice in this soup till it is tender, flavour with pepper and salt, add a little milk boiled separately, and serve grated Parmesan cheese with the soup.

Rice Soup à la Royale.—Take half a pound of rice and wash it thoroughly in several waters till the water ceases to be discoloured. Boil this rice in some stock that has been strongly flavoured with onion, carrot and celery, and strained off. When the rice is tender rub it through a wire sieve, then add some boiling milk, in which two or three bay-leaves have been boiled, and half a pint of cream, till the soup is a proper consistency. Serve some egg force-meat balls with the soup.

Sorrel Soup.—Take some sorrel and wash it very thoroughly. Like spinach, it requires a great deal of cleansing. Drain it off and place the sorrel in a stew-pan, and keep stirring it with a wooden spoon. When it has dissolved and boiled for two or three minutes, let it drain on a sieve till the water has run off. Next cut up a large onion and fry it in a little butter, but do not brown the onion. Add a tablespoonful of flour to every two ounces of butter used, also a teaspoonful of sugar, a little grated nutmeg, also a little pepper and salt; add the sorrel to this, with a small quantity of stock or water, then rub the whole through a wire sieve, and serve. In some parts of the Continent vinegar is added, but it is not adapted to English taste.

Sago Soup.—Take two ounces of sago, and having washed it very thoroughly, put it on to boil in a quart of stock strongly flavoured with onion, celery, and carrot, but which has been strained off. The sago must boil until it becomes quite transparent and tender. Flavour the soup with a little pepper and salt, a quarter of a nutmeg, grated, about half a teaspoonful of powdered sugar, and a teaspoonful of lemon juice from a hard lemon.

Sea-kale Soup.—This makes a very delicious soup, but it is somewhat rare. Take a bundle of sea-kale, the whiter the better. Throw it into boiling water, and let it boil for a few minutes, then take it out and drain it; cut it up into small pieces and place it in a stew-pan with about two ounces of butter, add a little pepper and salt and grated nutmeg; stir it up until the butter is thoroughly melted, but do not let it turn colour in the slightest degree. Add some milk, and let it simmer very gently for about half an hour. Rub the whole through a wire sieve, and add a small quantity of cream. Serve with toasted or fried bread.

Scotch Broth.—Take two or three ounces of pearl barley, wash it, and throw it into boiling water, and let it boil for five or ten minutes. Then drain it off and throw away the water. This is the only way to get pearl barley perfectly clean. Then put on the barley in some stock or water, and let it boil for four hours, till it is tender. Then add to it every kind of vegetable that is in season, such as onion, celery, carrot, turnip, peas, French beans, cut up into small pieces, hearts of lettuces cut up. Flavour with pepper and salt and serve altogether. If possible add leeks to this soup instead of onion, and just before serving the soup throw in a brimming dessert-spoonful of chopped blanched parsley to every quart of soup. A pinch of thyme can also be added.

Spinach Soup.—Wash some young, freshly gathered spinach, cut it up with a lettuce, and, if possible, a few leaves of sorrel, and throw them into boiling water. Let them boil for five minutes, drain them off, and throw them into cold water in order to keep their colour. Next take them out of the water and squeeze all the moisture from them; then melt two ounces of butter in a stew-pan, and add two tablespoonfuls of flour. When this is thoroughly mixed together, and begins to frizzle, add the spinach, lettuce, &c., and stir them round and round in the stew-pan till all is well mixed together. Then add sufficient water or vegetable stock to moisten the vegetables (add also a pinch of thyme), and let it boil. When it has boiled for about twenty minutes add a quart of milk that has been boiled separately, flavour with pepper and salt, and serve.

Tapioca Soup.—Clear tapioca soup is made by thickening some ordinary clear soup (*see* CLEAR SOUP) with tapioca, allowing about two ounces of tapioca to every quart. The tapioca should be put into the soup when it is cold, and it is then far less likely to get lumpy. Tapioca can also be boiled in a little strongly flavoured stock that has not been coloured, and then add some boiling milk. Tapioca should be allowed to simmer for an hour and a half. Of course, a little cream is a great improvement when the soup is made with milk.

Tomato Soup.—This is a very delicate soup, and the endeavour should be to try and retain the flavour of the tomato. Slice up an onion, or better still two shallots, and fry them in a little butter, to which can be added a broken-up, dried bay-leaf, a saltspoonful of thyme, and a very small quantity of grated nutmeg. Fry these in a little butter till the onion begins to turn colour, and then add a dozen ripe tomatoes from which the pips have been squeezed. Moisten with a very little stock or water, and let them stew till they are tender, then rub the whole through a wire sieve. The consistency should be that of pea soup. Add a little butter to soften the soup, and flavour with pepper and salt.

Turnip Soup.—Cut up some young turnips into small pieces, throw them into boiling water, let them boil for a few minutes, take them out and strain them, and put them into a stew-pan with about two ounces of fresh butter; add a little salt and sugar. Let them stew in the butter (taking great care that they don't turn colour) till they become soft, then add sufficient boiling milk to moisten them, so that when rubbed through a wire sieve the soup will be of the consistency of pea soup. Serve fried or toasted bread with the soup.

Vegetable Marrow Soup.—Take a large vegetable marrow, peel it, cut it open, remove all the pips, and place it in a stew-pan with about two ounces of fresh butter. Add a brimming teaspoonful of powdered sugar, a little grated nutmeg, and pepper and salt. Keep turning the pieces of vegetable marrow over in the butter, taking care that they do not at all turn colour. After frying these pieces gently for five or ten minutes, add some boiling milk, and let the whole simmer gently till it can be rubbed through a wire sieve. Care must be taken not to get this soup too thin, as the vegetable marrow itself contains a large quantity of water. Season with pepper and salt, and serve fried or toasted bread with the soup.

Vegetable Soup.—(*See* JARDINIÈRE SOUP.)

Vermicelli Soup.—Take a quarter of a pound of vermicelli and break it up into small pieces, throw it into boiling water, and let it boil for five minutes to get rid of the dirt and floury taste, then throw it immediately into about a quart of clear soup. The vermicelli must be taken from the boiling water and thrown into the boiling soup at once. If you were to boil the vermicelli, strain it off, and put it by to add to the soup, you would find it would stick together in one lump and be spoilt.

Vermicelli Soup, White.—The vermicelli must be thrown into white soup instead of clear soup. (*See* WHITE SOUP.)

White Soup.—Just as in ordinary white soup the secret of success is to have some strongly reduced stock, so in vegetarian white soup it is essential that we should have a small quantity of liquid strongly impregnated with the flavour of vegetables. For this purpose, place an onion, the white part of a head of celery, and a slice of turnip in a stew-pan with a little butter, and fry them till they are tender without becoming brown. Now add sufficient water to enable you to boil them, and let the water boil away till very little is left. Now rub this through a wire sieve and add it to a quart of milk in which a couple of bay-leaves have been boiled. Thicken the soup with a little white roux, add a suspicion of nutmeg, and also, if possible, a little cream. Flavour with pepper and salt. Serve fried or toasted bread with the soup.

CHAPTER II.

SAUCES.

Sauce Allemande.—Take a pint of butter sauce—(*see* BUTTER SAUCE)—and add to it four yolks of eggs. In order to do this you must beat up the yolks separately in a basin and add the hot butter sauce gradually, otherwise the yolks of eggs will curdle and the sauce will be spoilt. In fact, it must be treated exactly like custard, and in warming up the sauce it is often a good plan, if you have no *bain-marie*, to put the sauce in a jug and place the jug in a saucepan of boiling water. The sauce should be flavoured with a little essence of mushroom if possible. Essence of mushroom can be made from the trimmings of mushrooms, but mushroom ketchup must not be used on account of the colour. Essence of mushroom can be made by placing the trimmings of mushrooms in a saucepan, stewing them gently, and extracting the flavour. The large black mushrooms, however, are not suited. In addition to this essence of mushroom, a little lemon juice—allowing the juice of half a lemon to every pint, should be added to the sauce, as well as a slight suspicion of nutmeg, a pint of sauce requiring about a dozen grates of a nutmeg. A little cream is a great improvement to this sauce, but is not absolutely necessary. The sauce should be perfectly smooth. Should it therefore contain any lumps, which is not unfrequently the case in butter sauce, pass the sauce through a sieve with a wooden spoon and then put it by in a *bain-marie*, or warm it up in a jug as directed.

Almond Sauce.—This is suitable for puddings. The simplest way of making it is to make, say half a pint of butter sauce, or, cheaper, thicken half a pint of milk with a little corn-flour, sweeten it with white sugar, and then add a few drops of essence of almonds. About a dozen drops will be sufficient if the essence is strong, but essence of almonds varies greatly in strength. The sauce can be coloured pink with a few drops of cochineal.

Almond Sauce (clear).—Thicken half a pint of water with a little corn-flour, sweeten it with white sugar, add a dozen drops of essence of almonds and a few drops of cochineal to colour it pink. The sauce is very suitable to pour over custard puddings made in a basin or cup and turned out on to a dish. It is also very cheap.

Apple Sauce.—Peel say a dozen apples; cut them into quarters; and be very careful in removing all the core, as many a child is choked through carelessness in this respect. Stew the apples in a little water till they become a pulp, placing with them half a dozen cloves and half a dozen strips of the yellow part only of the outside of the rind of a *fresh* lemon of the size and thickness of the thumb-nail; sweeten with brown sugar, that known as Porto Rico being the most economical. Add a small piece of butter before serving.

Arrowroot Sauce.—Thicken half a pint of water with about a dessertspoonful of arrowroot and sweeten it with white sugar. The sauce can be flavoured by rubbing a few lumps of sugar on the outside of a lemon, or with a few drops of essence of vanilla, or with the addition of a little sherry or spirit, the best spirit being rum. This sauce can, of course, be coloured pink with cochineal.

Artichoke Sauce.—Proceed exactly as if you were making artichoke soup, only make the purée thicker by using less liquid. A simple artichoke sauce can be made by boiling down a few Jerusalem artichokes to a pulp, rubbing them through a wire sieve, and flavouring with pepper and salt.

Asparagus Sauce.—Boil a bundle of asparagus and rub all the green, tender part through a wire sieve, till it is a thick pulp, flavour with a little pepper and salt, add a small piece of butter, and a little spinach extract (vegetable colouring sold in bottles) in order to give it a good colour.

Bread Sauce.—Take some dry crumb of bread, and rub through a wire sieve. The simplest plan is to turn the wire sieve upside down on a large sheet of paper. The bread must be stale, and stale pieces can be put by for this purpose. Next take, say, a pint of milk, and let it boil; then throw in the bread-crumbs and let them *boil* in the milk. This is the secret of good bread sauce. Add a dozen peppercorns, and place a whole onion in the saucepan containing the bread and milk, and place the saucepan beside the fire in order to allow the bread-crumbs to swell. It will be found that though at starting the bread sauce was quite thin and milky, yet after a time it becomes thick. Take out the onion, add a little piece of butter, stir it up, and serve. A little cream is a great improvement, but is not absolutely necessary. This sauce, though very simple, requires care. Many persons will probably recollect having met with bread sauce which in appearance resembled a poultice too much to be agreeable either to the palate or the eye.

Butter Sauce.—This is the most important of all the sauces with which we have to deal. The great mistake made by the vast majority of women cooks is that they will use milk. They thicken a pint of milk with a little butter and flour and then call it melted butter, and, as a rule, send to table enough for twenty persons when only two or three are dining. As butter sauce will be served with the majority of vegetables, we would call the attention of vegetarians to the fact that, as a rule, ordinary cookery-books take for granted that vegetables will be served with the meat. When therefore vegetables are served separately, and are intended to be eaten with bread as a course by themselves, some alteration must be made in the method of serving them. Again, vegetarians should bear in mind that, except in cases where poverty necessitates rigid economy, a certain amount of butter may be considered almost a necessity, should the meal be wished to be both wholesome and nourishing. Francatelli, who was *chef-de-cuisine* to the Earl of Chesterfield, and was also chief cook to the Queen and *chef* at the Reform Club, and afterwards manager of the Freemasons' Tavern, in writing on this subject observes :—" Butter sauce, or, as it is more absurdly called, melted butter, is the foundation of the whole of the following sauces, and requires very great care in its preparation. Though simple, it is nevertheless a very useful and agreeable sauce when properly made. So far from this being usually the case, it is too generally left to assistants to prepare, as an insignificant matter; the result is therefore seldom satisfactory. When a large quantity of butter sauce is required, put four ounces of fresh butter into a middle-sized stew-pan, with some grated nutmeg and minionette pepper; to these add four ounces of sifted flour, knead the whole well together, and moisten with a pint of cold spring water; stir the sauce on the fire till it boils, and after having kept it gently boiling for twenty minutes (observing that it be not thicker than the consistency of common white sauce), proceed to mix in one pound and a half of sweet fresh butter, taking care to stir the sauce quickly the whole time of the operation. Should it appear to turn oily, add now and then a spoonful of cold spring water; finish with the juice of half a lemon, and salt to palate; then pass the sauce through a tammy into a large *bain-marie* for use."

We have quoted the recipe of the late M. Francatelli in full, as we believe it is necessary to refer to some very great authority in order to knock out the prejudice from the minds of many who think that they not only can themselves cook, but teach others, but who are bound in the chains of prejudice and tradition which, too often, in the most simple recipes, lead them to follow in the footsteps of their grandmothers.

Real butter sauce can be made as follows, on a small scale :— Take a claret-glass of water, and about a small teaspoonful of flour mixed with rather more than the same quantity of butter, and mix this in the water over the fire till it is of the consistency of very thin gruel. If it is thicker than this, add a little more water. Now take any quantity of butter, and gradually dissolve as much as you can in this thin gruel, adding say half an ounce at a time, till the sauce becomes a rich oily compound. After a time, if you add too much butter, the sauce will curdle and turn oily, as described by Francatelli.

Of course, in everyday life it is not necessary to have the butter sauce so rich, still it is simply ridiculous to thicken a pint of milk, or a pint of water, with a little butter and flour, and then call it butter sauce or melted butter. Suppose we have a large white cabbage, like those met with in the West of England, and we are going to make a meal off it in conjunction with plenty of bread. Suppose the cabbage is sufficiently large for six persons, surely half a pound of butter is not an excessive quantity to use in making butter sauce for the purpose. Yet prejudice is such that if we use half a pound of butter for the butter sauce, housekeepers consider it extravagant. On the other hand, if the butter were placed on the table, and the six persons helped themselves, and ate bread and butter with the cabbage and finished the half-pound, it would not be considered extravagant. Of course, this is simply prejudice.

A simple way of making melted butter is as follows:— Take half a pint of cold water, put it in a saucepan, and add sufficient white roux, or butter and flour mixed, till it is of the consistency of thin gruel. Now gradually dissolve in this, adding a little piece at a time, as much butter as you can afford; add a suspicion of nutmeg, a little pepper and salt, and a few drops of lemon-juice from a fresh lemon, if you have one in use.

Butter, Melted, or Oiled Butter.—Melted butter, properly speaking, is rarely met with in this country, but is a common everyday sauce on the Continent. It is simply what it says. A piece of butter is placed in a little sauce-boat and placed in the oven till the butter runs to oil, and then sent to table with all kinds of fish, with which in our present work we have nothing to do; but it is also sent to table with all kinds of vegetables, such as French artichokes, &c.; sometimes a spoonful of French capers is added to the oiled butter.

Butter, Black, or Beurre Noir.—Take two ounces of butter, and dissolve it in a frying-pan, and let it frizzle till the butter turns a brown colour; then add a tablespoonful of French vinegar, a teaspoonful of chopped capers, a teaspoonful of Harvey's sauce, and a teaspoonful of mushroom ketchup. Let it remain on the fire till the acidity of the vinegar is removed by evaporation. This is a very delicious sauce, and can be served with Jerusalem artichokes boiled whole, fried eggs, &c.

Caper Sauce.—Make some butter sauce, and to every half-pint of sauce add a dessertspoonful of chopped French capers. If the sauce is liked sharp, add some of the vinegar from the bottle of capers.

Carrot Sauce.—Proceed exactly as in carrot soup, using less liquid.

Cauliflower Sauce.—Proceed exactly as in cauliflower soup, using less liquid.

Celery Sauce.—Proceed exactly as in celery soup, only using less liquid. The thicker this sauce is the better.

Cherry Sauce.—Take a quarter of a pound of dried cherries, and put them into a small stew-pan, with a dessertspoonful of black currant jelly, a small stick of cinnamon, with half a dozen cloves, and add rather less than half a pint of water, and let the whole simmer gently for about ten minutes, when you must take out the spices and send the rest to table.

N.B.—If wine is not objected to in cooking, it is a very good plan to add claret instead of water.

Chestnut Sauce.—Proceed as in making chestnut soup, using as little liquid as possible, so as to make the sauce thick.

Cinnamon Sauce.—The simplest way of making cinnamon sauce is to sweeten some butter sauce with some white sugar, and then add a few drops of essence of cinnamon. The sauce can be coloured pink with a little cochineal. A little wine is an improvement. The sauce can also be made by breaking up and boiling a stick of cinnamon in some water, and then using the water to make some butter sauce.

Cocoanut Sauce.—Grate the white part of a cocoanut very finely, and boil it till tender in a very small quantity of water; add about an equal quantity of white sugar as there was cocoanut; mix in either the yolk of an egg or a tablespoonful of cream. A little lemon juice is an improvement.

Cucumber Sauce.—Take two or three small cucumbers, peel them, slice them, and place them in a dish with a little salt, which has the effect of extracting the water. Now drain the pieces off and strain them in a cloth, to extract as much moisture as possible. Put them in a frying-pan with a little

c

butter; fry them very gently, till they begin to turn colour, then rub them through a wire sieve; moisten the pulp with a little butter sauce; add a little pepper, salt, and grated nutmeg and vinegar to taste.

Currant Sauce (Red).—Put a couple of tablespoonfuls of red currant jelly into a small stew-pan, with half a dozen cloves, a small stick of cinnamon, and the rind of an orange. Moisten with a little water, or still better, a little claret, strain it off, and add the juice of the orange.

Currant Sauce (Black).—Proceed exactly as in the above recipe, substituting black currant jelly for red.

Curry Sauce.—Take six large onions, peel them, cut them up into small pieces, and fry them in a frying-pan in about two ounces of butter. As soon as the onions begin to change colour, take a small carrot and cut it up into little pieces, and a sour apple. When the onions, etc., are fried a nice brown, add about a pint of vegetable stock or water and let the whole simmer till the vegetables are quite tender, then add a teaspoonful of Captain White's curry paste and a dessertspoonful of curry powder; now rub the whole through a wire sieve, and take care that all the vegetables go through. It is rather troublesome, but will repay you, as good curry sauce cannot be made without. The curry sauce should be sufficiently thick owing to the vegetables being rubbed through the wire sieve. Should therefore the onions be small, less water or stock had better be added. Curry sauce could be thickened with a little brown roux, but it takes away from the flavour of the curry. A few bay-leaves may be added to the sauce and served up whole in whatever is curried. For instance, if we have a dish of curried rice, half a dozen or more bay-leaves could be added to the sauce and served up with the rice.

There are many varieties of curry. In India fresh mangoes take the part of our sour apples. Some persons add grated cocoanut to curry, and it is well worth a trial, although on the P. and O. boats the Indian curry-cook mixes the curry fresh every day and uses cocoanut oil for the purpose. In some parts of India it is customary to serve up whole chillies in the curry, but this would be better adapted to a stomach suffering from the effects of brandy-pawnee than to the simple taste of the vegetarian.

Dutch Sauce.—This is very similar to Allemande Sauce. Take half a pint of good butter sauce, make it thoroughly hot, add two yolks of eggs, taking care that they do not curdle, a little pepper and salt, a suspicion of nutmeg, and about a tablespoonful of tarragon vinegar. Some persons instead of using tarragon vinegar add a little lemon juice, say the half of a fresh lemon to this quantity, and half a dozen fresh tarragon leaves, blanched—that is, dipped for a few seconds in boiling water—and then chopped very fine. The tarragon vinegar is much the simplest, as it is very difficult to get fresh tarragon leaves unless one has a good garden or lives near Covent Garden Market.

Dutch Sauce (Green).—Proceed exactly as above and colour the sauce a bright green with a little spinach extract (vegetable colouring, sold in bottles by all grocers).

Egg Sauce.—Take half a dozen eggs, put them in a saucepan with sufficient cold water to cover them. Put them on the fire and let them boil for ten minutes after the water boils. Take them out and put them into cold water and let them stand for ten minutes, when the shells can be removed; then cut up the six hard-boiled eggs into little pieces, add sufficient butter sauce to moisten them, make the whole hot, and serve.

N.B.—Inexperienced cooks often think that hard-boiled eggs are bad when they are not, owing to their often having a tinge of green colour round the outside of the yolk and to their emitting a peculiar smell when the shells are first removed while hot. All eggs contain a small quantity of sulphuretted hydrogen.

Fennel Sauce.—Blanch and chop up sufficient fennel to colour half a pint of butter sauce a bright green, add a little pepper, salt, and lemon juice, and serve.

German Sweet Sauce.—Take a quarter of a pound of dried cherries, a small saltspoonful of powdered cinnamon, and a few strips of lemon peel, and put them in a small saucepan with about a quarter of a pint of water, or still better, claret, if wine is allowed, and let them simmer on the fire gently for about half an hour; then rub the cherries through a wire sieve with the liquor—(of course, the lemon peel and cloves will not rub through)—and add this to a quarter of a pound of stewed prunes. This is a very popular sauce abroad.

Ginger Sauce.—The simplest way of making ginger sauce is to sweeten half a pint of butter sauce and then add a few drops of essence of ginger. A richer ginger sauce can be made by taking two or three tablespoonfuls of preserved ginger and two or three tablespoonfuls of the syrup in which they are preserved, rubbing this through a wire sieve, adding about an equal quantity of butter sauce, making the whole hot in a saucepan.

Gooseberry Sauce.—Pick and then stew some green gooseberries, just moistening the stewpan with a little water to prevent them burning. Rub the whole through a hair sieve in order to avoid having any pips in the sauce. Sweeten with a little Demerara sugar, as Porto Rico would be too dark in colour. Colour the sauce a bright green with a little spinach extract.

N.B.—It is a mistake to add cream to gooseberry sauce, which is distinct altogether from gooseberry fool. In Germany, vinegar is added to this sauce and it is served with meat.

Horse-radish Sauce.—Horse-radish sauce is made, properly speaking, by mixing grated horse-radish with cream, vinegar, sugar, made mustard, and a little pepper and salt. A very simple method of making this sauce is to substitute tinned Swiss milk for the cream and sugar. It is equally nice, more economical, and possesses this great advantage: a few tins of Swiss milk can always be kept in the store cupboard, whereas there is considerable difficulty, especially in all large towns, in obtaining cream without giving twenty-four hours' notice, and the result even then is not always satisfactory. Horse-radish sauce is very delicious, and its thickness should be entirely dependent upon the amount of grated horse-radish. Sticks of horse-radish vary so very much in size that we will say, grate sufficient to fill a teacup, throw this into a sauce tureen, mix a dessertspoonful of Swiss milk with a tablespoonful of vinegar and about two tablespoonfuls of milk and a teaspoonful of made mustard, add this to the horse-radish, and, if necessary, sufficient milk to make the whole of the consistency of bread sauce.

As the sauce is very hot, as a rule it is best not to add any pepper, which can be easily added afterwards by those who like it.

Indian Pickle Sauce.—Chop up two or three tablespoonfuls of Indian pickles, place them in a frying-pan with a quarter of a pint of water, and if the pickles are sour as well as hot, let them simmer some little time so as to get rid of the vinegar by evaporation. Then thicken the whole with some brown roux till the sauce is as thick as pea soup. The vinegar should be got rid of as much as possible. This is a very appetising dish with boiled rice and Parmesan cheese.

Italian Sauce.—This is an old-fashioned recipe taken from a book written in French, and published more than fifty years ago. Put into a saucepan a little parsley, a shallot, some mushrooms and truffles, chopped very finely, with a piece of butter about the size of a walnut. Let all boil gently for half an hour, add a spoonful of oil, and serve.

Maître d'Hôtel Sauce.—Maître d'Hôtel sauce is simply a lump of butter mixed with some chopped parsley, a little pepper and salt, and lemon juice.

Hot sauce is often called Maître d'Hôtel when chopped blanched parsley and lemon juice is added to a little white sauce.

Mango Chutney Sauce.—Take a couple of tablespoonfuls of Mango Chutney, moisten it with two or three tablespoonfuls of butter sauce, rub the whole through a wire sieve, and serve either hot or cold. Or the chutney can be simply chopped up fine and added to the butter sauce without rubbing through the wire sieve.

Mayonnaise Sauce.—This is the most delicious of all cold sauces. It is composed entirely of raw yolk of egg and oil, flavoured with a dash of vinegar. When made properly it should be of the consistency of butter in summer time. Many women cooks labour under the delusion that it requires the addition of cream. Mayonnaise sauce is made as follows :— Break an egg and separate the yolk from the white, and place the yolk at the bottom of a large basin. Next take a bottle of oil, which must be cool but bright; if the oil is cloudy, as it often is in cold weather, you cannot make the sauce. Nor can you if the oil has been kept in a warm place. Now proceed to let the oil drop, drop by drop, on the yolk of egg, and with a silver fork, or still better, a wooden one, beat the yolk of egg and oil quickly together. Continue to drop the oil, taking care that only a few drops drop at a time, especially at starting, and continue to beat the mixture lightly and quickly. Gradually the yolk of egg and oil will begin to get thick, first of all like custard. When this is the case a little more oil may be added at a time, but never more than a teaspoonful. As more oil is added, and the beating continues, the sauce gets thicker and thicker, till it is nearly as thick as butter in summer time. When it arrives at this stage no more oil should be added. A little tarragon vinegar may be added at the finish, or a little lemon juice. This makes the sauce whiter in colour. One yolk of egg will take a teacupful of oil. It is best to add pepper and salt when the salad is mixed. Mayonnaise sauce is by far the best sauce for lettuce salad. It will keep a day, but should be kept in a cool place, and the basin should be covered over with a moist cloth.

Mayonnaise Sauce, Green.—Make some mayonnaise sauce as above, and colour it with some spinach colouring (vegetable colouring, sold in bottles by all grocers).

Mint Sauce.—Take plenty of fresh mint leaves, as the secret of good mint sauce is to have plenty of mint. Chop up sufficient mint to fill a teacup, put this at the bottom of a sauce tureen, pour sufficient boiling water on the mint to thoroughly moisten it, and add a tablespoonful of brown sugar, which dissolves best when the water is hot. Press the mint with a tablespoon to extract the flavour, let it stand till it is quite cold, and then add three or four tablespoonfuls of malt vinegar, stir it up, and the sauce is ready. The quantity of vinegar added is purely a matter of taste, but a teaspoonful of chopped mint floating in half a pint of vinegar is no more mint sauce than dipping a mutton chop in a quart of boiling water would be soup in ordinary cookery.

Mushroom Sauce, White.—Mushroom sauce can be made from fresh mushrooms or tinned mushrooms. When made from fresh they must be small button mushrooms, and not those that are black underneath. They must be peeled, cut up small, and have a little lemon juice squeezed over them to prevent them turning colour, or they had still better be thrown into lemon juice and water. They must now be fried in a frying-pan with a small quantity of butter till they are tender, and then added to a little thickened milk, or still better, cream. When made from tinned mushrooms, simply chop up the mushrooms, reserving the liquor, then add a little cream and thicken with a little white roux. A little pepper and salt should be added in both cases. Instead of using either milk or cream, you can use a small quantity of sauce Allemande.

Mushroom Sauce, Brown.—Proceed exactly as above with regard to the mushrooms, both fresh and tinned, only instead of adding milk, cream, or Allemande sauce, add a little stock or water, and then thicken the sauce with a little brown roux.

Mushroom Sauce, Purée.—Mushroom sauce, both white and brown, is sometimes served as a purée. It is simply either of the above sauces rubbed through a wire sieve.

Mustard Sauce.—Make, say, half a pint of good butter sauce, add to this a tablespoonful of French mustard and a tablespoonful of made English mustard. Stir this into the sauce, make it hot, and serve.

N.B.—French mustard is sold ready-made in jars, and is flavoured with tarragon, capers, ravigotte, &c.

Onion Sauce.—Take half a dozen large onions, peel them and boil them in a little salted water till they are tender. Then take them out and chop them up fine, and put them in a stew-pan with a little milk. Thicken the sauce with a little butter and flour, or white roux, and season with pepper and salt. A very nice mild onion sauce is made by using Spanish onions.

Onion Sauce, Brown.—Slice up half a dozen good-sized onions; put them in a frying-pan and fry them in a little butter till they begin to get brown, but be careful not to burn them, and should there be a few black pieces in the frying-pan, remove them; now chop up the onions, not too finely, and put them in a saucepan with a very little stock or water, let them simmer till they are tender, and then thicken the sauce with a little brown roux, and flavour with pepper and salt.

Orange Cream Sauce for Puddings.—Take a large ripe orange and rub a dozen lumps of sugar on the outside of the rind and dissolve these in a small quantity of butter sauce, and add the juice of the orange, strained. Now add a little cream, or half a pint of milk that has been boiled separately, in which case the sauce will want thickening with a little white roux. Rubbing the sugar on the outside of the rind of the orange gives a very strong orange flavour indeed—far more than the juice of almost any number of oranges would produce, so care must be taken not to overdo it. This is what French cooks call zest of orange.

Parsley Sauce.—Blanch and chop up sufficient parsley to make a brimming tablespoonful when chopped. Add this to half a pint of butter sauce, with a little pepper, salt, and lemon juice. It is very important to blanch the parsley, *i.e.*, throw it into a little boiling water before chopping.

Pine-apple Sauce.—Take a pine-apple, peel it, cut it up into little pieces on a dish, taking care not to lose any of the juice, place it in a saucepan with a very little water, just sufficient to cover the pine-apple; let it simmer gently until it is tender, and then add sufficient white sugar to make the liquid almost a syrup; a teaspoonful of corn-flour, made smooth in a little cold water, can be added; but the sauce should be of the consistency of syrup, and the corn-flour does away with the difficulty of making it too sickly. The juice of half a lemon may be added, and is, perhaps, an improvement.

Plum Sauce.—When made from ripe plums, take, say, a pound, and place them in a stew-pan with a very little water and a quarter of a pound of sugar. Take out the stones and crack them. Throw the kernels into boiling water so that you can rub off the skin, and add them to the sauce after you have rubbed the stewed plums through a wire sieve.

To make plum sauce from dried French plums proceed exactly as in making Prune Sauce. (*See* PRUNE SAUCE.)

Poivrade Sauce.—Take an onion, a very small head of celery, and a carrot, and cut them into little pieces, and put them into a frying-pan with a little butter, a saltspoonful of thyme, one or two dried bay-leaves, and about a quarter of a grated nutmeg and two or three sprigs of parsley. Fry these till they turn a light-brown colour, then add a little stock or water, and two tablespoonfuls of vinegar. Let this boil in the frying-pan for about half an hour, till the liquid is reduced in quantity. Thicken it with a little brown roux, and rub it through a wire sieve, make it hot, and serve. If wine is allowed, the addition of a little sherry is a great improvement to this sauce.

Prune Sauce.—Take a quarter of a pound of prunes, put them in a stew-pan with just sufficient water to cover them, and let them stew. Put in one or two strips of lemon-peel to stew with them, add a teaspoonful of brown sugar, about sufficient powdered cinnamon to cover a shilling, and the juice of half a lemon. When the prunes are quite tender take out the strip of lemon-peel and stones, rub the whole through a wire sieve, and serve.

Radish Sauce.—Take a few bunches of radishes and grate them, and mix this grated radish with a little oil, vinegar, pepper, and salt. You can colour the sauce red by adding a little beetroot, and make the sauce hot by adding a little grated horse-radish. This cold sauce is exceedingly nice with cheese. These *grated* radishes are more digestible than radishes served whole.

Raspberry Sauce.—This sauce is simply stewed raspberries rubbed through a wire sieve and sweetened. Some red-currant juice should be added to give it a colour. It is very nice made hot and then added to one or two beaten-up eggs and poured over any plain puddings, such as boiled rice, &c.

Ratafia Sauce.—Add a few drops of essence of ratafia to some sweetened arrowroot or to some butter sauce. The sauce can be coloured pink with a few drops of cochineal.

Ravigotte Sauce.—Put a tablespoonful each of Harvey's sauce, tarragon vinegar, and chilli vinegar into a small sauce-pan, and let it boil till it is reduced to almost one-half in quantity, in order to get rid of the acidity. Now add about half a pint of butter sauce, and throw in a tablespoonful of chopped blanched parsley.

Robert Sauce.—Take a couple of onions, cut them up into small pieces, and fry them with about an ounce of butter in a frying-pan. Drain off the butter and add a couple of tablespoonfuls of vinegar to the frying-pan, and let it simmer for ten minutes or a quarter of an hour so as to get rid of the acidity of the vinegar. Now add a very little stock or water, stir it up, and thicken the sauce with a little brown roux. Add a dessertspoonful of fresh mustard and a little pepper and salt.

Soubise Sauce.—Sauce Soubise is simply white onion sauce, rubbed through a wire sieve, and a little cream added. It is more delicate than ordinary onion sauce, and is often served in France with roast pheasant. It owes its name to a famous French general.

Sorrel Sauce.—Put about a quart of fresh green sorrel leaves (after being thoroughly washed) into an enamelled saucepan, with a little fresh butter, and let the sorrel stew till it is tender. Rub this through a wire sieve, add a little powdered sugar and a little lemon juice; a little cream may be added, but is not absolutely essential.

Sweet Sauce.—Take half a pint of butter sauce, and sweeten it with a little sugar. It can be flavoured by rubbing a little sugar on the outside of a lemon, or with vanilla, essence of almonds, or any kind of sweet essence. A little wine, brandy, or, still better, rum, is a great improvement. Some persons add cream.

Tarragon Sauce.—Blanch a dozen tarragon leaves, chop them up, and stew them in any kind of stock thickened with brown roux.

Tartar Sauce.—Take two or three tablespoonfuls of mayonnaise sauce, and add to this a brimming teaspoonful of chopped blanched parsley, as well as a piece of onion or shallot about as big as the top of the thumb down to the first joint, chopped very fine, and a brimming teaspoonful of French mustard. Mix the whole well together.

N.B.—A teaspoonful of anchovy sauce would be a great improvement were anchovy sauce allowed in vegetarian cookery.

Tomato Sauce.—The great secret of tomato sauce is to taste nothing but the tomato. Take a dozen ripe tomatoes, cut off the stalks, and squeeze out the pips, and put them in a stew-pan with a little butter, and let them stew till they are tender, and then rub the whole through a wire sieve. This, in our opinion, is the best tomato sauce that can be made, the only seasoning being a little pepper and salt. This wholesome and delicious sauce can, however, be spoilt in a variety of ways—by the addition of mace, cloves, shallots, onions, thyme, &c. It can also be made very unwholesome by the addition of a quantity of vinegar.

Truffle Sauce.—This sauce is very expensive if made from whole fresh truffles, but can be made more cheaply if you can obtain some truffle chips or parings. These must be stewed in a little stock, thickened with brown roux, and then rubbed through a wire sieve, a little sherry being a great improvement if wine is allowed.

Vanilla Sauce.—Add some essence of vanilla to some sweetened butter sauce.

White Sauce.—White sauce is sometimes required for vegetables and sometimes for puddings. In the former case some good-flavoured, uncoloured stock must be thickened with white roux, and then have sufficient cream added to it to make the sauce a pure white.

When white sauce is wanted for puddings, sufficient butter sauce must be sweetened, and very slightly flavoured with nutmeg or almond, and then an equal quantity of cream added to it to make it a pure white. White sauce should not have with it any strong predominant flavour.

CHAPTER III.

SAVOURY RICE, MACARONI, OATMEAL, &c.

RICE.

PROBABLY all persons will admit that rice is a too much neglected form of food in England. When we remember how small a quantity of rice weekly is found sufficient to keep alive millions and millions of our fellow-creatures in the East, it seems to be a matter of regret that rice as an article of food is not more used by the thousands and thousands of our fellow creatures in the East—not in the ordinary acceptation of the term, but East of Temple Bar. Rice is cheap, nourishing, easily cooked, and equally easily digested, yet that monster, custom, seems to step in and prevent the bulk of the poor availing themselves of this light and nourishing food solely for the reason that, as their grandfathers and grandmothers did not eat rice before them, they do not see any reason why they should, like the Irishman who objected to have his feet washed on the same ground. Of the different kinds of rice Carolina is the best, the largest, and the most expensive. Patna rice is almost as good; the grains are long, small, and white, and it is the best rice for curry. Madras rice is the cheapest.

Rice, pure and simple, is the food most suited for hot climates and where a natural indolence of disposition results in one's day's work of an ordinary Englishman being divided among twenty people. As we move towards more temperate zones it will be found the universal custom to qualify it by mixing it with some other substance; thus, though rice is largely eaten in Italy, it is almost invariably used in conjunction with Parmesan cheese. Rice contains no flesh-forming properties whatever, as it contains no nitrogen; and with all due respect to vegetarians, it will be found that as we recede from the Equator and advance towards the Poles our food must of necessity vary with the latitude, and, whereas we may start on a diet of rice, we shall be forced, sooner or later, to depend upon a diet of pemmican, or food of a similar nature.

Rice, to Boil.—The best method of boiling rice is, at any rate, a much disputed point, if not an open question. There are as 'many ways almost of boiling rice as dressing a salad, and each one thinks his own way the best. We will mention a few of the most simple, and will illustrate it by boiling a small quantity that can be contained in a teacup. Of course, boiling rice is very much simplified if you want some rice-water as well as rice itself. Rice-water contains a great deal of nourishment, a fact which is well illustrated by the well-known story of the black troops who served in India under Clive, who, at the siege of Arcot, told Clive, when they were short of provisions, that the water in which the rice was boiled would be sufficient for them, while the more substantial grain could be preserved for the European troops. Take a teacupful of rice and wash the rice in several waters till the water ceases to be discoloured. Now throw the rice into boiling water, say a quart; let the rice boil gently till it is tender, strain off the rice and reserve the rice-water for other purposes. The time rice will take to boil treated this way would be probably about twenty minutes, but this time would vary slightly with the quality and size of the rice.

Many years ago we watched a black man boiling rice on board a P. and O. boat (the *Mizapore*); he proceeded as follows:—He boiled the rice for about ten minutes, or perhaps a minute or two longer, strained it off in a sieve, and then washed the rice with cold water, and then put the rice back in the stew-pan to once more get hot and swell. Of course, this rice was being boiled for curry, and certainly the result was that each grain was beautifully separated from every other grain. We do not think, however, that this method of boiling rice is customary on all the boats of the P. and O. Company. Of course this method of boiling rice was somewhat wasteful.

By far the most economical method of boiling rice is as follows; and we would recommend it to all who are in the habit of practising economy on the grounds of either duty or necessity. Wash thoroughly, as before, a teacupful of rice and put it in a small stew-pan or saucepan with two breakfastcupfuls of water, bring this to a boil and let it boil for ten minutes, then remove the saucepan to the side of the fire and let the rice soak and swell for about twenty minutes. After a little time, you can put a cloth on the top of the saucepan to absorb the steam, similar to the way you treat potatoes after having strained off the water.

In boiling rice we must remember that there are two ways in which rice is served. One is as a meal in itself, the other as an accompaniment to some other kind of food. It will be found in Italy and Turkey and in the East generally, where rice forms, so to speak, the staff of life, that it is not cooked so soft and tender as it is in England, where it is generally served with something else. In fact, each grain of rice may be said to resemble an Irish potato, inasmuch as it has a heart in it. In Ireland potatoes, as a rule, are not cooked so much as they are in most parts of England. Probably the reason of this is, in most cases, that experience has taught people that there is more stay in rice and potatoes when served in a state that English people would call "under-done." There is no doubt that the waste throughout the length and breadth of this prosperous land through over-cooking is something appalling.

Another very good method of boiling rice is the American style. Take a good-sized stew-pan or saucepan that has a tight-fitting lid. Put a cloth over the saucepan, after first pouring in, say, a pint of water; push down the cloth, keeping it tight, so as to make a well, but do not let the cloth reach the water; wash the rice as before, and put on the lid tight. Of course, with the cloth the lid will fit very tight indeed. Now put the saucepan on the fire and make the water boil continuously. By these means you steam the rice till it is tender and lose none of the nourishment. We can always learn from America.

Risotto à la Milannaise.—Take a teacupful of rice, wash it thoroughly and dry it. Chop up a small onion and put it in the bottom of a small stew-pan and fry the onion to a light-brown colour. Now add the dry rice, and stir this up with the onion and butter till the rice also is fried of a nice light-brown colour. Now add two breakfastcupfuls of stock or water and a pinch of powdered saffron, about sufficient to cover a threepenny-piece; let the rice boil for ten or eleven minutes, move the saucepan to the side of the fire and let it stand for twenty minutes or half an hour till it has absorbed all the stock or water. Now mix in a couple of tablespoonfuls of grated Parmesan cheese. Flavour with a little pepper and salt, and serve the whole very hot.

Rice with Cabbage and Cheese.—Wash some rice and let it soak in some hot water, with a cabbage sliced up, for about an hour; then strain it off and put the rice and cabbage in a stew-pan with some butter, a little pepper and salt, and about a quarter of a grated nutmeg. Toss these about in the butter for ten minutes or a quarter of an hour over the fire, but do not let them turn colour; then add a small quantity of water or stock, let it stew till it is tender, and then serve it very hot with some grated cheese sprinkled over the top.

N.B.—The end of cheese rind can be utilised with this dish.

Rice with Cheese.—Wash some rice and then boil it for ten or eleven minutes in some milk, and let it stand till it has soaked up all the milk. The proportion generally is, as we have said before, a teacupful of rice to two breakfast-cupfuls of milk; but as we shall want the rice rather moist on the present occasion, we must allow a little more milk. Now mix in some grated cheese and a little pepper and salt, place the mixture in a pie-dish, and cover the top with grated cheese, and place the pie-dish in the oven and bake till the top is nicely browned, and then serve.

Some cooks add a good spoonful of made mustard to the mixture. Some persons prefer it and some don't; it is therefore best to serve some made mustard with the rice and cheese at table. Unless the mixture was fairly moist before it was put into the pie-dish, it would dry up in the oven and become uneatable.

Rice, Curried.—Boil a teacupful of well-washed rice in two breakfastcupfuls of water, and let the rice absorb all the water; put a cloth in the saucepan, and stir up the rice occasionally with a fork till the grains become dry and separate easily the one from the other. Now mix it up with some curry sauce, make the whole hot, and send it to table with a few whole bay-leaves mixed in with the rice. Only sufficient curry sauce should be added to moisten the rice—it must not be rice swimming in gravy; or you can make a well in the middle of the boiled rice and pour the curry sauce into this.

Rice Borders (Casseroles).—Casseroles, or rice borders, form a very handsome dish. It consists of a large border made of rice, the outside of which can be ornamented and the centre of which can be filled with a macedoine (*i.e.*, a mixture) of fruit or vegetables. As you are probably aware, grocers have in their shop-windows small tins with copper labels, on which the word is printed "Macedoine." This tin contains a mixture of cut-up, cooked vegetables. These are very useful to have in the house, as a nice dish can be served at a few moments' notice. Mixed fruits are also sold in bottles under the name of Macedoine of Fruits. Of course, both vegetables and fruit can be prepared at home much cheaper from fresh fruit and vegetables, but this requires time and forethought. These mixtures are very much improved in appearance when served in a handsomely made rice border, and as the border is eaten with the vegetables and fruit there is no want of economy in the recipe. Suppose we are going to make a rice border. Take a pound of rice and wash it carefully; if we are going to fill it with fruit we must boil it in sweetened milk, but if we are going to fill it with vegetables we must boil it in vegetable stock or water. Add, as the case may be, sufficient liquid to boil the rice till it is thoroughly tender and soft. Now place it in a large bowl, and with a wooden spoon mash it till it becomes a sort of firm, compact paste; then take it out and roll it into the shape of a cannon-ball, and having done this, flatten it till it becomes of the shape of the cheeses one meets with in Holland—flat top and bottom, with rounded edges. You can now ornament the outside by making it resemble a fluted mould of jelly. The best way of doing this is to cut a carrot in half and scoop out part of the inside with a cheese-scoop, so that the width of the part where it is scooped is about the same as the two flat sides. Make the outside of the rice perfectly smooth with the back of a wooden spoon. Butter the carrot mould to prevent it sticking, and press this gently on the outside of the shape of rice till it resembles the outside of a column in Gothic architecture, then place it in the oven and let it bake till it is firm and dry. Then scoop out the centre and put it back for a short time. If the border is going to be used for a macedoine of vegetables, beat up a yolk of egg and paint the outside of the casserole with this, and then it will bake a nice golden-brown colour. Now take it out of the oven and fill it accordingly. It can be served hot or cold, or it can be filled with a German salad. (*See* MACEDOINE OF FRUIT; MACEDOINE OF VEGETABLES; SALAD, GERMAN.)

Rice Croquettes, Savoury.—Boil a teacupful of rice in some stock or water (about two breakfastcupfuls), till it is tender, and until the rice has absorbed all the water or stock. Chop up a small onion very fine, fry it till tender in a very little butter, but do not let it brown; add a small teaspoonful of mixed savoury herbs, a brimming teaspoonful of chopped parsley, to the contents of the frying-pan for two or three minutes, and then add them to the rice. Mix it well together, and let the rice dry in the oven till the mixture is capable of being rolled into balls. Now take two eggs, separate the yolk from the white of one, beat up the whole egg and one white thoroughly in a basin, but do not beat it to a froth; add the rice mixture to this, mix it again very thoroughly, and then roll it into balls about the size of a small walnut, seasoning the mixture with sufficient pepper and salt. Roll these balls in flour, in order to insure the outside being dry, and roll them backwards and forwards on the sieve in order to get rid of the superfluous flour. Make some very fine bread-crumbs from some stale bread; next beat up the yolk of egg with about a dessertspoonful of warm water. Dip the rice-balls into this, and then cover them with the bread-crumbs. Let them stand for an hour or two for the bread-crumbs to get dry, and then fry them a light golden-brown colour in a little oil. Fried parsley can be served with them.

Instead of bread-crumbs you can use up broken vermicelli —the bottom of a jar of vermicelli can sometimes be utilised this way. This has a very pretty appearance. The vermicelli browns quickly, and the croquettes have the appearance of little balls covered in brown network.

Rice, Savoury.—There are several ways of serving savoury rice. The rice can be boiled in some stock, strongly flavoured with onion and celery, and when cooked sufficiently tender one or two eggs can be beaten up with it, pepper and salt added, and the mixture served with grated cheese.

Rice can also be rendered savoury by the addition of chopped mushrooms, pepper and salt, and a little butter, and if a tin of mushrooms is used, the liquor in the tin should be added to the boiled rice, but in every case the rice should be made to absorb the liquor in which it is boiled. Eggs can again be added, as well as grated Parmesan cheese.

A cheap and quick way of making rice savoury is to mix it with a large tablespoonful of chutney; make it hot with a little butter, and add pepper—cayenne if preferred—and a little lemon-juice.

Rice can also be served as savoury by boiling it in any of the sauces that may be termed savoury in distinction to those that are sweet, given in the chapter entitled "Sauces."

Rice and Eggs.—Boil, say half a pound of rice, and let it absorb the water in which it is boiled. Take four hard-boiled eggs, separate the yolks from the whites, chop the whites very fine, and add them to the rice with about a brimming teaspoonful of chopped blanched parsley and sufficient savoury herbs to cover a sixpence. Put this in the saucepan and make it hot, with a little butter, and flavour with plenty of pepper and salt. In the meantime beat the yellow hard-boiled yolks to a yellow powder, turn out the rice mixture, when thoroughly hot, into a vegetable dish, and put the yellow powder either in the centre or make a ring of the yellow powder round the edge of the rice, and serve a little pile of fried parsley in the middle.

Rice and Tomato.—Take half-a-dozen ripe tomatoes, squeeze out the pips, and put them in a tin in the oven with a little butter to bake; baste them occasionally with a little butter. In the meantime boil half a pound of rice in a little stock or water, only adding sufficient so that the rice can absorb the liquid. When this is done (and this will take about the same time as the tomatoes take to bake), pour all the liquid and butter in the tin on to the rice and stir it well up with some pepper and salt. Put this on a dish, and serve the tomatoes on the rice with the red, unbroken side uppermost.

Macaroni.—Macaroni is a preparation of pure wheaten flour. It is chiefly made in Italy, though a good deal is made in Geneva and Switzerland. The best macaroni is made in the neighbourhood of Naples. The wheat that grows there ripens quickly under the pure blue sky and hot sun, and consequently the outside of the wheat is browner while the inside of the wheat is whiter than that grown in England. The wheat is ground and sifted repeatedly. It is generally sifted about five times, and the pure snow-white flour that falls from the last sifting is made into macaroni. It is first mixed with water and made into a sort of dough, the dough being kneaded in the truly orthodox Eastern style by being trodden out with the feet. It is then forced by a sort of rough machinery through holes, partially baked during the process, and then hung up to dry. Macaroni contains a great amount of nourishment, and it is only made from the purest and finest flour. It is the staple dish throughout Italy, and in whatever form or way it is cooked, except as a sweet, tomatoes and grated Parmesan cheese seem bound to accompany it.

Sparghetti.—Sparghetti is a peculiar form of macaroni. Ordinary macaroni is made in the form of long tubes, and when macaroni pudding is served in schools, it is often irreverently nicknamed by the boys gas-pipes. Sparghetti is not a tube, but simply macaroni made in the shape of ordinary wax-tapers, which it resembles very much in appearance. In Italy it is often customary to commence dinner with a dish of sparghetti, and should the dinner consist as well of soup, fish, entrée, salad, and sweet, the sparghetti would be served before the soup. Take, say, half a pound of sparghetti, wash it in cold water, and throw it instantly into boiling salted water; boil it till it is tender, about twenty minutes, drain it, put it into a hot vegetable-dish, and mix in two or three tablespoonfuls of grated Parmesan cheese; toss it about lightly with a couple of forks, till the cheese melts and forms what may be called cobwebs on tossing it about. Add also two tablespoonfuls of tomato conserve (sold by all grocers, in bottles), and serve immediately. This is very cheap, very satisfying, and very nourishing; and it is to be regretted that this popular dish is not more often used by those who are not vegetarians, who would benefit both in pocket and in health were they to lessen their butcher's bill by at any rate commencing dinner, like the Italians, with a dish of sparghetti.

Macaroni—Italian Fashion.—This is very similar to sparghetti, only ordinary pipe macaroni is used. Take, say, a teacupful of macaroni, wash it, break it up into two-inch pieces, and throw it into boiling water that has been salted. Strain it off, and put it in the stew-pan for a few minutes, with a little piece of butter and some pepper and salt. Add a tablespoonful of tomato conserve, and serve it with some grated Parmesan cheese, served separate in a dish.

Some rub the stew-pan with a head of garlic. This gives it what may be called a more foreign flavour, but this should not be done unless you know your guests like garlic. Unfortunately, the proper use of garlic is very little understood in this country.

Macaroni Cheese.—Some years back this was almost the only form in which macaroni was served in this country. Macaroni cheese used to be served at the finish of dinner in a dried-up state, and was perhaps one of the most indigestible dishes which the skill, or want of skill, of our English cooks was able to produce. Wash and then boil a quarter of a pound of macaroni in a little milk till it is quite tender, then put into a well-buttered oval tin a layer of macaroni, and cover this with a layer of bread-crumbs, mixed with grated cheese, and add a few little lumps of butter; then put another layer of macaroni and another layer of bread-crumbs and cheese. Continue alternate layers till you pile up the dish, taking care to have a layer of dried bread-crumbs at the top. Warm some butter, but do not oil it, and pour some of this warm butter over the top of the dish to moisten them; put the dish in the oven till it is hot through, then take it out and brown the top quickly with a red-hot salamander. If you leave the macaroni cheese in the oven too long the dish will taste oily and the cheese get so hard as to become absolutely indigestible. Any kind of grated cheese will do for this dish, but to the English palate it is best when made from a moist cheese similar to that which would be used in making Welsh rabbit.

Macaroni and Eggs.—Take half a pound of macaroni and throw it into boiling water that has been salted. In the meantime have ready four hard-boiled eggs. When the macaroni is nearly tender throw the hard-boiled eggs into cold water for a minute, in order to enable you to take off the shells without burning your fingers. Cut the eggs in half, take out the half yellow yolk without breaking it; cut the whites of the eggs into rings and mix these rings with the macaroni on the dish. The macaroni and eggs must be flavoured with pepper and salt, and if possible pour a little white sauce over the whole. If you have no white sauce add a little cream or a little thickened milk with a little butter dissolved in it; now sprinkle a little chopped blanched parsley over the whole and ornament the dish with the eight half-yolks.

Macaroni à la Reine.—Boil half a pound of pipe macaroni. Meanwhile warm slowly in a saucepan three-quarters of a pint of cream, and slice into it half a pound of Stilton or other white cheese, add two ounces of good fresh butter, two blades of mace, pounded, a good pinch of cayenne and a little salt. Stir until the cheese is melted and the whole is free from lumps, when put in the macaroni and move it gently round the pan until mixed and hot, or put the macaroni on a hot dish and pour the sauce over. It may be covered with fried bread-crumbs of a pale colour and browned in a Dutch oven.

Macaroni au Gratin.—Break up a pound of macaroni in three-inch lengths, boil as usual and drain. Put into a stew-pan a quarter of a pound of fresh butter, the macaroni, twelve ounces of Parmesan and Gruyère cheese mixed, and about a quarter of a pint of some good sauce, white sauce. Move the stew-pan and its contents over the fire until the macaroni has absorbed the butter, etc., then turn it out on a dish, which should be garnished with croutons of fried bread. Pile it in the shape of a dome, cover with bread-raspings, a little clarified butter run through a colander, and brown very lightly with a salamander.

N.B.—The above two recipes are taken from "Cassell's Dictionary of Cookery."

Macaroni as an Ornament.—Macaroni is sometimes used to ornament the outside of puddings, either savoury or sweet. Suppose the pudding has to be made in a small round mould or basin. Some pipe macaroni is boiled in water till it is tender, and then cut up into little pieces a quarter of an inch in length. The inside of the mould is first thickly buttered, and then these little quarter-inch tubes are stuck in the butter close together; the pudding, for instance a custard pudding, is then poured into the mould and the mould steamed. When the pudding is turned out the outside of the pudding has the appearance of a honey-comb, and looks extremely pretty. The process is not difficult, but rather troublesome, as it requires time and patience.

Macaroni, Timbale of.—This is a somewhat expensive dish. You have first to decorate a plain mould with what is called *nouilles* paste, which is made by mixing half a pound of flour with five yolks of eggs. The mould is then lined with ordinary short paste, made with half a pound of flour, a quarter of a pound of butter, and one yolk of egg, mixed in the ordinary way. When the mould is lined, you have to fill it up with flour, and bake it in a moderate oven for about an hour. You then take it out, empty out the flour and brush it well out with an ordinary brush and dry the mould in a very slack oven. The mould is then filled with some macaroni that has been boiled tender in milk and flavoured with vanilla and sugar and Parmesan cheese. The macaroni must be so managed that it absorbs the moisture. The mould is filled, made hot, and then turned out. It is customary to shake some powdered sugar over the mould, and then glaze it with a red-hot salamander.

N.B.—Very few kitchens possess a proper salamander, but if you make the kitchen shovel red-hot it will be found to answer the same purpose.

Macaroni in Scollop Shells.—Take half a pound of

macaroni, wash it, and throw it into boiling water. Take the macaroni out, drain it, and throw it into cold water. Then take it out and cut it into pieces not more than half an inch in length. Take about a quarter of a pound of butter, melt it in a stew-pan, and add about a cupful of milk, or still better, cream. Stir it and dredge in enough flour to make it thick, or still better, thicken it with a little white roux; now add some pepper and salt, about a quarter of a grated nutmeg, two or three spoonfuls of grated Parmesan cheese; add the cut-up macaroni and stir the whole well up over the fire together and fill the scollop shells with the mixture, and throw some grated cheese over the top. Bake the scollops in the oven till the cheese begins to brown; then pour a little oiled butter over the top of the cheese. If made with cream this dish is somewhat rich, but forms an admirable meal eaten with plenty of bread.

Macaroni Nudels.—The word nudel is probably derived from French *nouilles* paste. It is made in a similar manner, or nearly so. French cooks use only yolk of egg and flour. English cooks use beaten-up eggs, and sometimes even reserve the yolks for other purposes and make the paste with white of egg. In any case, the yolks, the whole eggs, or the white without the yolks, must be well beaten up and then mixed in with the flour with the fingers till it makes a stiff paste. This paste or dough is then rolled out with a straight rolling pin—(not an English one)—till it is as thin as a wafer. The board must be well floured or it will stick. A marble slab is best, and if you are at a loss for a rolling-pin try an empty black bottle. It is very important to roll the pastry thin, and it has been well observed that the best test of thinness is to be able to read a book through the paste. When rolled out, let each thin cake dry for five or ten minutes. If you have a box of cutters you can cut this paste into all sorts of shapes according to the shape of the cutters, or you can cut each thin cake into pieces about the same size, and then with a sharp dry knife cut the paste into threads. These threads or ornamental shapes can be thrown into boiling clear soup, when they will separate of their own accord. Nudel paste is, in fact, home-made Italian paste, or, when cut into threads, home-made vermicelli. It is very nourishing, as it is made with eggs and flour.

Macaroni, Savoury.—Take half a pound of macaroni and boil it in some slightly salted water, and let it boil and simmer till the macaroni is tender and absorbs all the water in which it is boiled. Now take a dessertspoonful of raw mustard, *i.e.*, mustard in the yellow powder. Mix this gradually with the macaroni, and add five or six tablespoonfuls of grated Parmesan cheese and a little cayenne or white pepper according to taste. Turn the mixture out on to a dish, sprinkle some more grated Parmesan cheese over the top, bake it in the oven till it is slightly brown, pour a little oiled butter on the top, and serve.

Macaroni and Chestnuts.—Bake about twenty chestnuts till they are tender, and then peel them and pound them in a mortar, with a little pepper and salt and butter, till they are a paste. Next wash and boil in the ordinary way half a pound of macaroni. Drain off the macaroni and put it in a stew-pan with the chestnuts and about a couple of ounces of butter to moisten it, and stir it all together and put an onion in to flavour it as if you were making bread sauce; but the onion must be taken out whole before it is served. If the mixture gets too dry, it can be moistened with a little milk or stock. After it has been stirred together for about a quarter of an hour, turn it out on to a dish, cover it with a little Parmesan cheese, bake in the oven till it is brown, and moisten the top when browned with a little oiled butter.

Macaroni and Tomatoes.—Take half a pound of macaroni; wash it and boil it until it is tender. In the meantime take half a dozen or more ripe tomatoes; cut off the stalks, squeeze out the pips, and place them in a tin in the oven with a little butter to prevent their sticking. It is as well to baste the tomatoes once or twice with the butter and the juice that will come from them. Put the macaroni when tender and well drained off into a vegetable-dish, pour the contents of the tin, butter and juice, over the macaroni and add pepper and salt, and toss it lightly together. Now place the whole tomatoes on the top of the macaroni, round the edge, at equal distances. It is a great improvement to the appearance of the dish to sprinkle a little chopped blanched parsley over the macaroni. The tomatoes should be placed with the smooth, red, unbroken side uppermost.

Macaroni and Cream.—Boil half a pound of macaroni; cut it up into pieces about two inches long and put it into a stew-pan with two ounces of butter and a quarter of a pound of grated cheese, composed of equal parts of Gruyère and Parmesan cheese. Moisten this with about three tablespoonfuls of cream. Toss it all lightly together till the cheese makes cobwebs. Add a little pepper and salt and serve with some fried bread round the edge cut up into ornamental shapes. Carefully made pieces of toast, cut into triangles, will do instead of the fried bread.

Tagliatelli.—Take some flour and water, and with the addition of a little salt make a paste which can be rolled out quite thin; cut this into shapes of the breadth of half a finger. Throw them into boiling water and let them boil a few minutes. Then remove them to cold water; drain them on a sieve and use them as macaroni; place at the bottom of a dish some butter and grated cheese, then a layer of *tagliatelli* seasoned with pepper, another layer of butter and cheese, and then one of *tagliatelli*, until the whole is used; pour over it a glass of cream, add a layer of cheese, and finish like macaroni cheese, browning it in the oven.

Oatmeal Porridge.—Of all dishes used by vegetarians there are none more wholesome, more nourishing, or more useful as an article of everyday diet for breakfast than oatmeal porridge. When we remember that the Scotch, who, for both body and brain, rank perhaps first amongst civilised nations, almost live on this cheap and agreeable form of food, we should take particular pains in the preparation of a standing dish which is in itself a strong argument in favour of a vegetarian diet when we look at the results, both mentally and bodily, that have followed its use North of the Tweed. The following excellent recipe for the preparation of oatmeal porridge is taken from a book entitled, "A Year's Cookery," by Phyllis Browne (Cassell & Co.) :—" When there are children in the family it is a good plan, whatever they may have for breakfast, to let them begin the meal either with oatmeal porridge or bread-and-milk. Porridge is wholesome and nourishing, and will help to make them strong and hearty. Even grown-up people frequently enjoy a small portion of porridge served with treacle and milk. Oatmeal is either 'coarse,' 'medium,' or 'fine.' Individual taste must determine which of these three varieties shall be chosen. Scotch people generally prefer the coarsest kind. The ordinary way of making porridge is the following—Put as much water as is likely to be required into a saucepan with a sprinkling of salt, and let the water boil. Half a pint of water will make a single plateful of porridge. Take a knife (a 'spurtle' is the proper utensil) in the right hand, and some Scotch, or coarse, oatmeal in the left hand, and sprinkle the meal in gradually, stirring it briskly all the time; if any lumps form draw them to the side of the pan and crush them out. When the porridge is sufficiently thick (the degree of thickness must be regulated by individual taste), draw the pan back a little, *put on the lid*, and let the contents simmer gently till wanted; if it can have two hours' simmering, all the better; but in hundreds of families in Scotland and the North of England it is served when it has boiled for ten minutes or a quarter of an hour; less oatmeal is required when it can boil a long time, because the simmering swells the oatmeal, and so makes it go twice as far. During the boiling the porridge must be stirred frequently to keep it from sticking to the saucepan and burning, but each time this is done the lid must be put on again. When it is done enough it should be poured into a basin or upon a plate, and served hot with sugar or treacle and milk or cream. The very best method that can be adopted for making porridge is to soak the coarse Scotch oatmeal in water for *twelve hours*, or more (if the porridge is wanted for breakfast it may be put into a pie-dish over night, and left till morning). As soon as the fire is lighted in the morning it should be placed on it, stirred occasionally, kept covered, and boiled as long as possible, although it may be served when it has boiled for twenty minutes. When thus prepared it will be almost like a delicate jelly, and acceptable to the most fastidious palate. The proportions for porridge made in this way are a heaped tablespoonful of coarse oatmeal to a pint of water.

"It is scarcely necessary to give directions for making—

"Bread and Milk, for everyone knows how this should be done. It may be said that the preparation has a better appearance if the bread is cut very small before the boiling milk is poured on it, and also that the addition of a small pinch of salt takes away the insipidity. Rigid economists sometimes swell the bread with boiling water, then drain this off and pour milk in its place. This, however, is almost a pity, for milk is so very good for children; and though recklessness is seldom to be recommended, a mother might well be advised to be reckless about the amount of her milk bill, provided always that the quantity of milk be not wasted, and that the children have it."

Milk Porridge.—Take a tablespoonful of oatmeal and mix it up in a cup with a little cold milk till it is quite smooth, in a similar way as you would mix ordinary flour and milk in making batter. Next put a pint of milk on to boil, and as soon as it boils mix in the oatmeal and milk, and let it boil for about a quarter of an hour, taking care to keep stirring it the whole time. The fire should not be too fierce, as the milk is very apt to burn. Flavour this with either salt or sugar.

Rice and Barley Porridge.—Take a quarter of a pound of rice and a quarter of a pound of Scotch barley and wash them very thoroughly. The most perfect way of washing barley and rice is to throw them into boiling water, let them boil for five or ten minutes, and then strain them off. By this means the dirty outside is dissolved. Next boil the rice and barley gently for three or four hours, strain them off, and boil them up again in a little milk for a short time before they are wanted. It will often be found best to boil the barley for a couple of hours and then add the rice. A little cream is a very great improvement. The porridge can be flavoured with pepper and salt, but is very nice with brown sugar, treacle, or jam, and when cold forms an agreeable accompaniment to stewed fruit.

Whole-meal Porridge.—Boil a quart of water and gradually stir in about half a pound of whole-meal; let it boil for about a quarter of an hour, and serve. Cold milk should accompany this porridge.

Lentil Porridge.—To every quart of water add about six

tablespoonfuls of lentil flour; let the whole boil for about a quarter of an hour, and flavour with pepper and salt.

Hominy.—Take a teacupful of hominy, wash it in several waters and rub it well between the hands, and throw away the grains that float on the top, the same as you do with split peas, pour the water off the top, then strain it off, and put it in a basin with a quart of water, and cover the basin over with a cloth; put it by to soak overnight, should it be required for breakfast in the morning. The next day put it in an enamelled stew-pan with about a teaspoonful of salt, and let it simmer gently over the fire, taking care that it does not burn. It is best to butter the bottom of the saucepan, or if you have a small plate that will just go inside you will find this a great protection. Let it simmer gently for rather more than an hour. Stir it well up and flavour it with either sugar or salt, and let it be eaten with cold milk poured on it on the plate, or with a little butter.

The hominy should simmer until it absorbs all the water in which it is boiled. As a rule a good teacupful will absorb a quart.

Hominy, Fried.—This is made from the remains of cold boiled hominy. When cold it will be a firm jelly. Cut the cold hominy into slices, flour them, egg and bread-crumb them, and then plunge them into some smoking hot oil till they are of a nice bright golden colour. They are very nice eaten with lemon-juice and sugar, or they can be served with orange marmalade.

Frumenty.—Take a quarter of a pint of wheat, wash it thoroughly, and let it soak for twelve hours or more in water. Strain it off and boil it in some milk till it is tender, but do not let it get pulpy. As soon as it is tender add a quart of milk, flavoured with a little cinnamon, three ounces of sugar, three ounces of carefully washed grocer's currants, and let it boil for a quarter of an hour. Beat up three yolks of eggs in a tureen, and gradually add the mixture. It must not be added to the eggs in a boiling state or else they will curdle. A wineglassful of brandy is a great improvement, but is not absolutely necessary. The wheat takes a long time to get tender, probably four hours.

Sago Porridge.—Wash the sago in cold water and boil it in some water, allowing about two tablespoonfuls to every pint; add pepper and salt and let cold milk be served with the porridge.

Milk Toast.—This is a very useful way of using up stale bread. Toast the bread a light brown, and if by chance any part gets black scrape it gently off. Butter the toast slightly, lay the toast on the bottom of a soup-plate, and pour some boiling milk over it. Very little butter should be used, and children often prefer a thin layer of marmalade to butter.

CHAPTER IV.

EGGS (SAVOURY) AND OMELETS.

Eggs, Plain Boiled.—There is an old saying that there is reason in the roasting of eggs. This certainly applies equally to the more common process of boiling them. There are few breakfast delicacies more popular than a new-laid egg. There are few breakfast indelicacies more revolting than the doubtful egg which makes its appearance from time to time, and which may be classed under the general heading of "Shop 'uns." It is a sad and melancholy reflection that these more than doubtful "shop 'uns" were all *once* new-laid. It is impossible to draw any hard-and-fast line to say at what exact period an egg ceases to be fit for boiling. There is an old tradition, the truth of which we do not endorse, that eggs may arrive at a period when, though they are not fit to be boiled, fried, poached, or hard-boiled, they are still good enough for puddings and pastry. There is no doubt that many good puddings are spoilt because cooks imagine they can use up doubtful eggs.

When eggs are more than doubtful, they are often bought up by the smaller pastry-cooks in cheap and poor neighbourhoods of our large towns, such as the East-End of London. These eggs are called "spot eggs," and are sold at thirty and forty a shilling. They utilise them as follows: They hold the egg up in front of a bright gas-light, when the small black spot can be clearly seen. This black spot is kept at the lowest point of the egg, *i.e.*, the egg is held so that this black spot is at the bottom. The upper part of the egg is then broken and poured off, the black spot being retained. The moment the smallest streak proceeds from this black spot the pouring-off process is stopped. Of course, the black part is all thrown away, the stench from it being almost intolerable, containing, as it does, sulphuretted hydrogen. We mention the fact for what it is worth. It would be a bold man who tried to lay down any law as to where waste ceases and the use of wrongful material commences. Everything depends upon the circumstances of the case in question. We fear there are many thousands, hundreds of thousands, in this great city of London, whose everyday life more or less compares with that of a shipwrecked crew. They "fain would fill their belly with the husks that the swine do eat, but no man gives unto them." There is this to be said in favour of vegetarian diet—that, were it universal, grinding poverty would be banished from the earth. We must not cry out too soon about using what some men call bad material. Lord Byron, when he was starving after shipwreck, was glad to make a meal off the paws of his favourite dog, which had been thrown away when the carcase had been used on a former occasion.

The simplest way of boiling eggs is to place them at starting in boiling water, and boil them from three to three and a half to four minutes, according to whether they are liked very lightly boiled, medium, or well-set.

The egg saucepan should be small, so that when the eggs are first plunged in it takes the water off the boil for a few seconds, otherwise the eggs are likely to crack. This applies more particularly to French eggs, which have thin, brittle shells containing an excess of lime, probably due to the large quantity of chalk which is the distinguishing feature of the soil in the *Pas de Calais*, which is the chief neighbourhood from which French eggs are imported.

Over a million eggs are imported from France to England *every day*, notwithstanding the fact that thousands are kept awake by the crying of their neighbours' fowls.

There is a strange delusion among Londoners that an egg is not good if it is milky. This, of course, is never met with in London, for the simple reason that a milky egg means, as a rule, than it has not been laid more than a few hours. For this reason eggs literally hot from the nest are not suitable for making puddings or even omelets. Eggs that have been kept one or two days will be found to answer better, as they possess more binding properties.

There is an old-fashioned idea that the best way to boil an egg is to place it in the saucepan in cold water, to put the saucepan on the fire, and as soon as the water boils the egg is done. A very little reflection will show that this entirely depends upon the size of the saucepan and the fierceness of the fire. If the saucepan were the size of the egg, the water would boil before the egg was hot through; on the other hand, no one could place an egg in the copper on this principle and then light the copper fire.

Eggs are best boiled in the dining-room on the fire, or in an ornamental egg-boiler. By this means we get the eggs *hot*, an occurrence almost unknown in large hotels and big establishments.

Eggs, To Break.—Whenever you break eggs, never mind what quantity, always break each egg separately into a cup first; see that it is good, and then throw it into a basin with the rest. One bad egg would spoil fifty. Supposing you have a dozen or two dozen new-laid eggs just taken from the nest, it is not an uncommon thing to have one that has been overlooked for weeks, and which may be a half-hatched mass of putrefaction.

Eggs, Fried.—The first point is to have a clean frying-pan, which is an article of kitchen furniture very rarely indeed met with in this country. For frying eggs, and for making omelets, it is essential that the frying-pan should never be used for other purposes.

If you think *your* frying-pan is perfectly clean, warm it in front of the fire for half a minute, put a clean white cloth over the top of the finger, and then rub the inside of the frying-pan.

To fry eggs properly, very little butter will be required; a little olive-oil will answer the same purpose. If you have too much "fat," the white of the eggs are apt to develop into big bubbles or blisters. Another point is, you do not want too fierce a fire. Fry them very slowly. Some cooks will almost burn the bottom of the egg before the upper part is set. As soon as the white is set round the edge, you will often find the yolk not set at all, surrounded by a rim of semi-transparent "albumen." When this is the case, it is very often a good plan to take the frying-pan off the fire (we are presuming the stove is a shut-up one), and place it in the oven for a minute or so, leaving the oven door open. By this means the heat of the oven will set the upper part of the eggs, and there is no danger of the bottom part being burnt.

There is a great art in taking fried eggs out of a frying-pan and serving them on a dish. Fried eggs, to look nice, should have the yolk in the centre, surrounded by a ring of white, perfectly round, rather more than an inch in breadth.

Take an egg-slice in the *left* hand, slide it under each egg separately, so that the yolk gets well into the middle of the slice. Now take a knife in the right hand and trim off the superfluous white. By this means you will be able to do it neatly. The part trimmed away is virtually refuse. Of course, you do not throw away more than is necessary, but take care that the white rim round the yolk is of uniform breadth. Most cooks take the egg out with their right hand, and attempt to trim it with the left; the result is about as neat as what would happen were you to attempt to write a letter with your left hand in a hurry.

Very often the appearance of fried eggs is improved by sprinkling over them a few specks of chopped parsley.

In placing fried eggs on toast, place the slice over the toast and draw the slice away. Do not push the egg on; you may break it.

Eggs, Poached.—The best kitchen implement to use for poaching eggs is a good large frying-pan. The mistake is to let the water boil; it should only just simmer. You should avoid having the white of the egg set too hard. We should endeavour to have the eggs look as white as possible. In order to insure this, put a few drops of vinegar or lemon-juice into the water, break the eggs separately into a cup, and then turn them very gently into the hot water. When they are set fairly firm take them out with an egg-slice, using the left hand as before, and trim them with the right. It is not necessary, in poached eggs, to have a clear yolk surrounded with a white uniform ring. Poached eggs often look best when the yolk reposes in a sort of pillow-case of white. Before putting them on toast or spinach, &c., be very careful to drain off the water; this is particularly important when the water is acid, especially with vinegar.

Eggs, Hard-boiled.—Place the eggs in cold water, bring

D

the water to boiling point, and let them boil for ten minutes; if the hard-boiled eggs are wanted hot, put them in cold water for half a minute, in order that you may remove the shells without burning your fingers. If the eggs are required cold, it is best not to remove the shells till just before they are wanted; but if they have to be served cold, similar to what we meet with at railway refreshment-rooms, let them be served cold, *whole*. If you cut a hard-boiled egg the yolk very soon gets discoloured and brown round the edge, shrivels up, and becomes most unappetising in appearance.

Eggs, Curried.—Take some hard-boiled eggs, cut them in halves (remove the half-yolks), and cut them into rings. Place all these rings round the edge of the dish, and pile the white rings up to make a sort of border; pour some thick curry sauce in the middle, place the half-yolks at equal distances apart, on the white round the edge, and sprinkle a few specks of green parsley round the edge on the whites; this will give the dish a pretty appearance.

Eggs, Devilled.—Take, say, half a dozen eggs, boil them hard, remove the shells while hot, cut them in halves, scoop out the yolk, and cut a tiny piece off the bottom of each white cup, so that it will stand upright—à la Columbus. Next take all the yolks, and put them in a basin, and pound them with a little butter till you get a thick squash; add some cayenne pepper, according to taste, a little white pepper, a little salt, and a few drops of chilli-vinegar or ordinary vinegar; you can also add a little finely chopped parsley— say a teaspoonful. Fill each cup with some of this mixture, and as there will be more than enough to fill them, owing to the butter, bring them to a point, like a cone. Devilled eggs are best served cold, in which case they look best placed on a silver or ordinary dish, the bottom of which is covered with green parsley; the white looks best on a green bed. Some cooks chop up the little bits of white cut off from the bottom of the cups, divide them into two portions, and colour one half pink by shaking them in a saucer with a few drops of cochineal. These white and pink specks are then sprinkled over the parsley.

N.B.—In an ordinary way devilled eggs require anchovy

sauce to be mixed with the yolks, but anchovy sauce is not allowed in vegetarian cookery.

Eggs à la bonne femme.—Proceed exactly as in making devilled eggs, till you place the yolks in the basin; then add to these yolks, while hot, a little dissolved butter, and small pieces of chopped cold boiled carrot, turnip, celery, and beet-root; season with white pepper and salt, and mix well together. Add also a suspicion of nutmeg and a little lemon-juice. Fill the cups with this while the mixture is moist, as when the butter gets cold the mixture gets firm. If you use chopped beet-root as well as other vegetables, it is best to fill half the cups with half the mixture before any beetroot is added, then add the beet-root and stir the mixture well up and it will turn a bright red. Now fill the remaining half of the cups, and place them on the dish containing the parsley, alternately. The red contrasts prettily with the light yellowish white of the first half. Do not colour the white specks with cochineal, as this is a different shade of red from the beet-root. You can chop up the white and sprinkle it over the parsley with a little chopped beet-root as well.

Eggs à la tripe.—Small Spanish onions are perhaps best for this dish, but ordinary onions can be used. Cut the onions cross-ways after peeling them, so that they fall in rings, and remove the white core. Two Spanish or half a dozen ordinary onions will be sufficient. Fry these rings of onions in butter till they are tender, without browning them. Take them out of the frying-pan and put them aside. Add a spoonful of flour to the frying-pan, and make a paste with the butter, and then add sufficient milk so that when it is boiled and stirred up it makes a thick sauce; add pepper and salt, a little lemon-juice, and a small quantity of grated nutmeg. Put back the rings of onions into this, and let them simmer gently. Take half a dozen hard-boiled eggs, cut the eggs in halves, remove the yolks, and cut the whites into rings, like the onions, mixing these white egg-rings with the onions and sauce; make the whole hot and serve on a dish, using the hard-boiled half-yolks to garnish; sprinkle a little chopped parsley over the whole, and serve.

Egg, Forcemeat of, or Egg Balls.—Take three hard-boiled

yolks of eggs, powder them, mix in a raw yolk, add a little pepper and salt, a small quantity of grated nutmeg, about a saltspoonful of finely chopped parsley, chopped up with a pinch of savoury herbs, or a pinch of dust from bottled savoury herbs, sifted from them, may be added instead. Roll these into balls not bigger than a very small marble, flour them, and throw them into boiling water till they are set.

In many parts of the Continent, hard-boiled yolks of eggs, served whole, are used as egg balls. A much cheaper way of making egg balls is as follows:—Beat up one egg, add a teaspoonful of chopped blanched parsley, some pepper and salt, and a very little grated nutmeg. Sift a bottle of ordinary mixed savoury herbs in a sieve, and take about half a saltspoonful of the dust and mix this with the egg, This will be found really better than using the herbs themselves. Now make some very fine bread-crumbs from *stale* bread, and mix this with the beaten-up egg till you make a sort of soft paste or dough; roll this into balls the size of a marble, flour them, and throw them into boiling water. The balls must be small or they will split in boiling.

Eggs au gratin.—Make about half a pint of butter sauce, make it hot over the fire, and stir in about two ounces of Parmesan cheese, a quarter of a nutmeg grated, some white pepper, and the juice of half a lemon. Make this hot, and then add the yolks of four eggs. Stir it all up, and keep stirring very quickly till the mixture begins to thicken, when you must instantly remove it from the fire, but continue stirring for another minute. In the meantime have ready some hard-boiled eggs, cut these into slices, and make a circle of the bigger slices on a dish; then spread a layer of the mixture over the slices of egg, and place another layer on this smaller than the one below, then another layer of mixture, and so on with alternate layers till you pile it up in the shape of a pyramid. Spread a layer of the remainder of the mixture over the surface, and sprinkle some powdered light-coloured bread-raspings mixed with some grated Parmesan cheese over the whole; place the dish in the oven to get hot and to slightly brown, and then serve. Some fried bread cut into pretty shapes can be used to ornament the base.

Eggs and Spinach.—Make a thick purée of spinach; take some hard-boiled eggs, cut them in halves while hot, after removing the shells, and press each half a little way into the purée, so that the yellow yolk will be shown surrounded by the white ring. Be very careful not to smear the edge with the spinach.

N.B.—Sometimes eggs are poached and laid on the spinach whole.

Eggs and Turnip-tops.—Proceed exactly as above, using a purée of turnip-tops instead of spinach.

Eggs and Asparagus.—Have ready some of the green parts of asparagus, boiled tender, and cut up into little pieces an eighth of an inch long so that they look like peas. Beat up four eggs very thoroughly with some pepper and salt, and mix in the asparagus, only do not break the pieces of green. Melt a couple of ounces of butter in a small stew-pan, and as soon as it commences to froth pour in the beaten-up egg and asparagus; stir the mixture quickly over the fire, being careful to scrape the bottom of the saucepan. As soon as the mixture thickens pour it on some hot toast, and serve.

Eggs and Celery.—Have ready some stewed celery on toast. (*See* CELERY, STEWED.) Poach some eggs and place them on the top. Hard-boiled eggs, cut into slices, can be added to the celery instead of poached eggs.

When stewed celery is served as a course by itself, the addition of the eggs and plenty of bread make it a wholesome and satisfying meal.

Egg Salad.—(*See* SALADS.)

Egg Sandwiches.—(*See* SANDWICHES.)

Egg Sauce.—(*See* SAUCES.)

Egg Toast.—Beat up a couple of eggs, melt an ounce of butter in a saucepan, and add to it a little pepper and salt. As soon as the butter begins to froth, add the beaten-up egg and stir the mixture very quickly, and the moment it begins to thicken pour it over a slice of hot buttered toast.

Eggs à la Dauphine.—Take ten hard-boiled eggs, cut them in halves and remove the yolks, and place the yolks in a basin with a piece of new bread, about as big as the fist, that has been soaked in some milk, or better still, cream; add a teaspoonful of chopped parsley, a quarter of a grated nutmeg, and two ounces of grated Parmesan cheese; rub the whole well together, and then add two whole eggs, well beaten up, to the mixture to moisten it. Next fill all these white cups of eggs with some of this mixture, place the eggs well together, and spread a thin layer of the mixture over the top; then take a smaller number of half-eggs, filled, and place on the top and make a pyramid, so that a single half-egg is at the top. You can place ten half-eggs at the bottom in one layer, six half-eggs on the top of these, spreading a thin layer of the mixture, then three half-eggs, one more layer of the mixture, and then one half-egg at the summit. This dish is sometimes ornamented by forcing hard-boiled yolks of eggs through a wire sieve. It falls like yellow vermicelli into threads. This dish should be placed in the oven, to be made quite hot, and some kind of white sauce should be poured round the edge.

Eggs and Black Butter.—Fry some eggs, serve them up on a hot dish, and pour some black butter round the base. (*See* BLACK BUTTER SAUCE.)

Eggs and Garlic.—This is better adapted for an Italian than an English palate. Take half a dozen heads of garlic and fry them in a little butter in order to remove the rankness of flavour. Take them out and pound them in a mortar with rather more than a tablespoonful of oil; heat this on the fire in a stew-pan, after adding some pepper and salt. Beat up an egg, and stir this in with the oil and garlic till the mixture gets thick. Arrange some slices of hard-boiled eggs—four eggs would be sufficient—pour this mixture in the centre, and serve.

Eggs with Mushrooms.—Take half a pint of button mushrooms and, if fresh, peel them and throw them instantly into water made acid with lemon-juice, in order that they may not turn a bad colour. In the meantime slice up a good-sized Spanish onion, and fry the onion in a little butter. As soon as the onion is a little tender, chop up and add the mushrooms. Put all this into a stew-pan with a little butter sauce, or a little water can be added and then thickened with a little butter and flour. Let this simmer gently for nearly half an hour, add a little made mustard, pepper and salt and a dessertspoonful of vinegar. Before sending to table add half a dozen hard-boiled eggs; the whites should be cut into rings, and should be only put into the sauce long enough to get hot; the yolks should be kept separate, but must be warmed up in the sauce.

Eggs and Onions.—Cut up a large Spanish onion in slices, and fry it in some butter till it is a light brown and tender, but do not let it burn; drain off the butter and put the fried onion on a dish; sprinkle some cayenne pepper and a little salt over the onions, and squeeze the juice of a whole lemon over them. Now poach some eggs and serve them on the top of the onion.

Eggs and Potatoes.—Take the remains of some floury potatoes, beat up an egg, and mix the potato flour with the egg. You can also chop up very finely a small quantity of onion and parsley, and season with plenty of pepper and salt. The respective quantities of floury potatoes and beaten egg must be so regulated that you can roll the mixture into balls without their having any tendency to break. Make the balls big enough so that when you press them between the hands you can squeeze the ball into the shape of an ordinary egg, or you can mould them into this shape with a tablespoon. Now flour these imitation eggs in order to dry the surface, and then dip them into well-beaten-up egg and cover them with dried bread-crumbs, and fry them in a little butter or oil, or brown them in the oven, occasionally basting them with a little butter.

Eggs and Sauce Robert.—Take some hard-boiled eggs, cut them into quarters, and make them hot in some Sauce Robert—(*see* ROBERT SAUCE)—and serve with fried or toasted bread in a dish.

Eggs and Sorrel.—Make a thick purée of sorrel—(*see* SORREL SAUCE)—and serve some hard-boiled or poached eggs on the top.

Eggs, Broiled.—Cut a large slice of crumb of bread off a big loaf; toast it lightly, put some pieces of butter on it, and put it on a dish in front of the fire; then break some eggs carefully on to the toast, and let them set from the heat of the fire like a joint roasting; when the side nearest the fire gets set, it will be necessary to turn the dish round. When the whole has set, squeeze the juice of an orange over the eggs, and a little grated nutmeg may be added. The eggs and toast should be served in the same dish in which they are baked.

Eggs, Buttered.—Break some eggs into a flat dish, then take a little butter and make it hot in a frying-pan till it frizzles and begins to turn brown. Now pour this very hot butter, which is hotter than boiling water, over the eggs in the dish. Put the dish in the oven a short time, and finish off setting the yolks with a red-hot salamander.

Eggs, Scrambled.—Scrambled eggs, when finished properly, should have the appearance of yellow and white streaks, distinct in colour, but yet all joined together in one mass. Melt a little butter in the frying-pan, break in some eggs, as if for frying; of course, the whites begin to set before the yolks. As soon as the whites are nearly but not quite set, stir the whole together till the whole mass sets. By this means you will get yellow and white streaks joined together. It is very important that you don't let the eggs get brown at the bottom; you will therefore require a perfectly clean frying-pan and not too fierce a fire.

Eggs in Sunshine.—This is a name given to fried eggs with tomato served on the top. You want a dish that will stand the heat; consequently, take an oval baking-tin, or enamelled dish that you can put on the top of a shut-up stove. Melt a little butter in this, and as soon as it begins to frizzle break some eggs into the dish, and let them all set together. As soon as they are set, pour four or five tablespoonfuls of tomato conserve on the top; this is much better than tomato sauce, which contains vinegar. Or you can bake half a dozen ripe tomatoes in a tin in the oven, and place these on the top instead of the tomato conserve.

Eggs and Cucumber.—Peel and slice up two or three little cucumbers of the size generally sold on a barrow at a penny each. Put these with two or three ounces of butter in a stew-pan, and three small onions about the size of the top of the thumb, chopped very fine; fry these and add a dessert-spoonful of vinegar. When the cucumber is tender, and a little time has been allowed for the vinegar to evaporate, add six hard-boiled eggs, cut into slices; make these very hot and serve. Pepper and salt must be added.

Eggs with Cheese.—Take a quarter of a pound of grated cheese (the cheese should be dry and white), melt this cheese gently in a stew-pan over the fire, with a little bit of butter about as big as the thumb, in order to assist the cheese in melting. Mix with it a brimming teaspoonful of chopped parsley, two or three tiny spring onions, chopped very fine, and about a quarter of a small grated nutmeg. When the cheese is melted, add six beaten-up eggs, and stir the whole together till they are set. Fried or toasted bread should be served round the edge of the dish.

Little Eggs for Garnishing.—This is a nice dish when you require a lot of white of eggs for other purposes, such as icing a wedding-cake, or making light vanilla or almond biscuits.

Take six hard-boiled yolks, powder them, flavour with a little pepper and salt, and mix in three raw yolks; mix this well together, and roll them into shapes like very small sausages, pointed at each end like a foreign cigar. Flour these on the outside, and throw them into boiling water. These can be used for garnishing purposes for the vast majority of vegetarian dishes. They can be flavoured if wished with grated nutmeg, chopped parsley, and a few savoury herbs.

Omelets.—It is a strange fact, but not the less true, that to get a well-made omelet in a private house in this country is the exception and not the rule. A few general remarks on making omelets will, we hope, not be out of place in writing a book on an exceptional style of cookery, in which omelets should play a most important part.

First of all, we require an omelet-pan, and for this purpose the cheaper the frying-pan the better. The best omelet-pan of all is a copper one, tinned inside. Copper conveys heat quicker than almost any other metal; consequently, if we use an ordinary frying-pan, the thinner it is the quicker will heat be conveyed.

It is very essential that the frying pan be absolutely clean, and it will be found almost essential to reserve the omelet-pan for omelets only. A frying-pan that has cooked meat should not be used for the purpose; and although in vegetarian cookery a frying-pan has not been used in this manner, we should still avoid one in which onions or vegetables, or even black butter has been made. The inside of an omelet-pan should always look as if it had only just left the ironmonger's shop.

The next great question is, how much butter should be allowed for, say, six eggs? On this point the greatest authorities differ. We will first quote our authorities, and then attempt to give an explanation that reconciles the difference. A plain omelet may be roughly described as settings of eggs well beaten up by stirring them up in hot butter. One of the oldest cookery books we can call to mind is entitled "The Experienced English Housekeeper," by Elizabeth Raffald. The book, which was published in 1775, is dedicated to the Hon. Lady Elizabeth Warburton, whom the authoress formerly served as housekeeper. The recipe is entitled "To make an amulet." The book states, "Put a quarter of a pound of butter into a frying-pan, break six eggs"; Francatelli also gives four ounces of butter to six eggs.

On the other hand, Soyer, the great cook, gives two ounces of butter to six eggs; so also does the equally great Louis Eustache Ude, cook to Louis XVI.

We may add that "Cassell's Dictionary of Cookery" recommended two ounces of butter to six eggs, whilst "Cassell's Shilling Cookery" recommends four eggs.

The probable reason why two such undoubtedly great authorities as Soyer and Francatelli should differ is that in making one kind of omelet you would use less butter than in making another. Francatelli wrote for what may be described as that "high class cooking suited for Pall Mall clubs," where no one better than himself knew how best to raise the jaded appetite of a wealthy epicure. Soyer's book was written for the people.

There are two kinds of omelets, one in which the egg is

scarcely beaten at all, and in which, when cooked, the egg appears set in long streaks. There is also the richer omelet, which is sent to table more resembling a light pudding. For the former of these omelets, two ounces of butter will suffice for six eggs; for the latter of these you will require four ounces of butter, or else the omelet will be leathery. In Holland, Belgium, and Germany, and in country villages in France, the omelet is made, as a rule, with six eggs to two ounces of butter. It comes up like eggs that have been set. In the higher-class restaurants in Paris, like Bignon's, or the Café Anglais, the omelet is lighter, and probably about four ounces of butter would be used to six eggs.

This probably explains the different directions given in various cookery books for making omelets.

Omelet, Plain.—Melt *four* ounces of butter in a frying-pan, beat up six eggs *till they froth;* add a little pepper and salt, pour the beaten-up eggs into the frying-pan as soon as the butter begins to frizzle, and with a tablespoon keep scraping the bottom of the frying-pan in every part, not forgetting the edge. Gradually the mixture becomes lumpy; still go on scraping till about two-thirds or more are lumpy and the rest liquid. Now slacken the heat slightly by lifting the frying-pan from the fire, and push the omelet into half the frying-pan so that it is in the shape of a semicircle. By this time, probably, it will be nearly set. Take the frying-pan off the fire, and hold it in a slanting direction in front of the fire. When the whole is set, as it will quickly do, slide off the omelet from the frying-pan on to a hot dish with an egg-slice, and serve.

Omelet, Plain (another way).—Put *two* ounces of butter into a frying-pan, break six eggs into a basin with a little pepper and salt, *and beat them very slightly*, so that the yolks and whites are quite mixed into one, but do not beat them more than you can help, and *do not let the eggs froth*. As soon as the butter frizzles, pour in the beaten eggs, scrape the frying-pan quickly with a spoon in every part till the mixture gets lumpy. Now slacken the heat if the fire is fierce, and let the mixture set in the frying-pan like a pancake. As soon as it is nearly set, with perhaps only a dessertspoonful of liquid left unset, turn the omelet over, one half on to the other half, in the shape of a semicircle, and bring the spoonful of unset fluid to join them over the edge. Slide off the omelet on to a hot dish with an egg-slice.

Omelet with Fine Herbs.—Chop up a dessertspoonful of parsley, and add a good pinch of powdered savoury herbs, add these with pepper and salt to the six beaten-up eggs in a basin. Beat up the eggs, either slightly or very thoroughly, according to whether you use two ounces of butter or four. Proceed in every respect, in making the omelet, as directed for plain omelet above.

Omelet with Onion.—Proceed exactly as in the above recipe, only adding to the chopped parsley a piece of onion or shallot about as big as the top of the thumb down to the first joint, also very finely chopped. When onion is used in making an omelet a little extra pepper should be added.

Omelet with Cheese.—Proceed as if making an ordinary omelet, with four ounces of butter. Add to the six well beaten-up eggs about four ounces of grated Parmesan cheese; a small quantity of cream will be found a great improvement to this omelet. A little pepper and salt must, of course, be added as well.

Potato Omelet.—Mix three ounces of a floury potato with six eggs, a little pepper and salt, .and half a pint of milk, and make the milk boil and then stand for a couple of minutes before it is mixed with the eggs; pour this mixture into three or four ounces of butter, and proceed as in making an ordinary omelet.

Potato Omelet, Sweet.—Proceed exactly as above, only instead of adding pepper and salt mix in a brimming tablespoonful of finely powdered sugar, the juice of a lemon, with half a grated nutmeg.

Cheese Soufflé.—To make a small cheese soufflé in a round cake-tin, proceed as follows :—Make the tin very hot in the oven. Put in about an ounce of butter, so as to make the tin oily in every part inside. The tin must be tilted so that the butter pours round the sides of the tin as well as the bottom. Take two eggs, separate the yolks from the whites, and beat the whites to a stiff froth; beat up the two yolks very thoroughly with a quarter of a pint of milk. Add to this two tablespoonfuls of grated Parmesan cheese; add this mixture to the beaten-up whites, and mix the whole carefully together. Now pour this mixture into the hot buttered tin, which should be five or six inches deep, and bake it in the oven. The mixture will rise to five or six times its original depth. As soon as it is done, run with the soufflé from the oven door to the dining-room door. However quick you may be, the soufflé will probably sink an inch on the way. Some cooks wrap hot flannel on the outside of the tin to keep up the heat. If you have a folded dinner napkin round the tin for appearance sake, as is usually the case, fold the napkin before you make the soufflé, and make the napkin sufficiently big round that it can be dropped over the tin in an instant. The napkin should be pinned, and be quite half an inch in diameter bigger than the width of the tin. This is to save time. Delay in serving the soufflé is fatal.

Omelet Soufflé, Sweet.—In making an omelet soufflé, sweet, you can proceed in exactly the same manner as making a cheese soufflé, with the exception that you add two tablespoonfuls of powdered sugar instead of two tablespoonfuls of grated cheese. The omelet will, however, require flavouring of some kind, the two most delicate being vanilla and orange-flower water. You can flavour it with lemon by rubbing a few lumps of sugar on the outside of a lemon, and then pounding this with the powdered sugar. It must be pounded very thoroughly and mixed very carefully, or else one part of the omelet will taste stronger of lemon than the other. Some powdered sugar should be shaken over the top of the soufflé just before serving.

Omelet Soufflé (another way).—When a soufflé is made on a larger scale, and served up on a flat dish, it is best to proceed as follows:—Take six ounces of powdered sugar, and mix them with six yolks of eggs and a dessertspoonful of flour and a pinch of salt. To this must be added whatever flavouring is used, such as vanilla. This is all mixed together till it is perfectly smooth. Next beat the six whites to a very stiff froth; mix this in with the batter lightly, put two ounces of butter into an omelet-pan, and as soon as the butter begins to frizzle pour in the mixture. As it begins to set round the edges, turn it over and heap it up in the middle, and then slide the omelet off on to a plated edged baking dish, which must be well buttered. Put it in the oven for about a quarter of an hour, to let it rise, shake some powdered sugar over the top, and serve very quickly.

Omelet, Sweet.—Make an ordinary plain omelet with six eggs and either two or four ounces of butter, as directed for making omelet, plain. Instead of adding pepper and salt to the beaten-up eggs, add one or two tablespoonfuls of finely powdered sugar. At the last moment, sprinkle a little powdered sugar over the omelet, and just glaze the sugar with a red-hot salamander.

Omelet with Jam.—Make a plain sweet omelet as directed above, adding rather less sugar—about half. If you make the omelet with two ounces of butter, and turn it over, put a couple of tablespoonfuls of jam on the omelet, and turn the half over the jam. It is best to put the jam in the oven for a minute or two to take the chill off.

If you make the omelet with four ounces of butter, you must put the jam by the side of the omelet and let the thin part of the omelet cover it. Of course, the question what jam is best for sweet omelet is purely a matter of taste. Most good judges consider that apricot jam is the best, and if the sweet omelet itself be flavoured with a little essence of vanilla, the result is generally considered one of the nicest sweets that can be sent to table. Strawberry jam, especially if some of the strawberries are whole, is also very nice. The objection to raspberry jam is the pips.

A most delicious omelet can be made by chopping up some preserved slices of pine-apple, and placing this in the omelet, and making the pine-apple syrup hot and pouring it round the base. Red-currant jelly, black-currant jam, and plum jam can all be used. One of the cheapest and, in the opinion of many, the best sweet omelets can be made with six eggs, two ounces of butter, and three or four tablespoonfuls of orange marmalade. In this case it will cost no more to rub a few lumps of sugar on the outside of an orange, and pound these with the powdered sugar you use to sweeten the omelet. If the marmalade is liquid, as it often is, one or two tablespoonfuls of the juice can be poured round the edge of the omelet.

Omelet au Rhum.—As a rule, spirits are not allowed in vegetarian cookery. An omelet au rhum is simply a sweet omelet, plain, with plenty of powdered sugar sprinkled over the top, with some rum ignited poured over it just before it is sent to table. The way to ignite the rum is to fill a large spoon, like a gravy-spoon, and hold a lighted wooden taper (not wax; it tastes) underneath the spoon till the rum lights. The dish should be hot. It may be a consolation to teetotallers to reflect that the fact of burning the rum causes all the alcohol to evaporate, and there is nothing left but the flavour.

Omelet au Kirsch.—Proceed as above, substituting Kirschenwasser for Rum.

Omelet, Vegetable.—A plain omelet can also be served with any purée of vegetables, so that we can have—Asparagus Omelet, Artichoke Omelet, French Bean Omelet, Celery Omelet, Spinach Omelet, Mushroom Omelet, Tomato Omelet, &c.

CHAPTER V.

SALADS AND SANDWICHES.

Salads and Sandwiches.—Probably the most patriotic Englishman will admit that, on the subject of salads, we can learn something from the French. During the last half-century a great improvement has taken place on this point in this country. Many years ago it was the fashion to dress an English lettuce, resembling in shape an old umbrella, with a mixture of brown sugar, milk, mustard, and even anchovy and Worcester sauce, and then add a few drops of oil, as if it were some dangerous poison, like prussic acid, not to be tampered with lightly. The old-fashioned lettuces were so hard and crisp that it was difficult to chew them without making a noise somewhat similar to walking on a shingly beach. In modern days, however, we have arrived at a stage of civilisation in which, as a rule, we use soft French lettuces instead of the hard gingham-shaped vegetables which somehow or other our grandfathers ate for supper with a whole lobster, seasoned with about half a pint of vinegar, and then slept none the worse for the performance. The first point for consideration, if we wish to have a good salad, is to have the lettuces crisp and dry. Old-fashioned French cookery-books direct that the lettuce should never be washed. The stalks should be cut off, the outside leaves removed and thrown away, and the lettuce itself should then be pulled in pieces with the fingers, and each piece wiped with a clean cloth. This is not always practicable, but the principle remains the same. You can wash the lettuce leaves without bruising them. You can dry them by shaking them up lightly in a large clean cloth, and you can spread them out and let them get *dry* an hour or two before they are dressed.

Another important point to be borne in mind is that a salad should never be dressed till just before it is wanted to be eaten. If by chance you put by the remains of a dressed salad, it is good for nothing the next morning. Finally, the oil must be pure olive oil of the best quality, and to ensure this it should bear the name of some well-known firm. A good deal of the oil sold simply as salad oil, bearing no name, is adulterated, sometimes with cotton-seed oil.

Salad, French Lettuce, Plain.—Clean one or more French lettuces (throw away all the leaves that are decayed or bruised), place these in a salad-bowl, and, supposing we have sufficient for two persons, dress the salad as follows:—Put a saltspoonful of salt and half a saltspoonful of pepper into a tablespoon. Fill the tablespoon up with oil, stir the pepper and salt up with a fork, and pour it over the lettuce. Now add another tablespoonful of oil, and then toss the lettuce leaves lightly together with a spoon and fork. Allow one tablespoonful of oil to each person. This salad would suffice for two. Be sure and mix the lettuce and oil well together before you add any vinegar. The reason of this is that if you add the vinegar first it would soak into the lettuce leaves, making one part more acid than another. Having well mixed up the lettuce and oil, add half a tablespoonful of vinegar. Mix it once more, and the salad is dressed.

In France they always add to the lettuce, before it is dressed, two or three finely chopped fresh tarragon leaves. Dried tarragon can be used, but it is not equal to fresh. If you have no tarragon it is a great improvement to use tarragon vinegar instead of ordinary vinegar. Tarragon vinegar is sold by all grocers at sixpence per bottle.

It is also often customary to rub the salad-bowl with a bead of garlic, or rub a piece of crust of bread with garlic, and toss this piece of crust up with the salad after it has been dressed. Garlic should never be chopped up, but only used as stated above.

A good French salad is also always decorated with one or more hard-boiled eggs, cut into quarters, longways. These are placed on the top of the lettuce.

Salad, English, Lettuce.—The ordinary English salad is made either with French or English lettuces, and is generally dressed as follows:—One or two tablespoonfuls of cream or milk, a teaspoonful of made mustard, two tablespoonfuls of vinegar, pepper, and salt. There are many people still living in remote parts of the country who prefer this style of dressing.

Salad, English, Mixed.—The old-fashioned English *mixed* salad generally consisted of English lettuce cut up into strips crossways, to which was added mustard and cress, boiled beet-root, chopped celery, spring onions, radishes, and watercress. It is by no means a bad mixture when dressed with oil, and, of course, it can be dressed à l'Anglaise. It makes an excellent accompaniment to a huge hunk of cheese, a crusty loaf, a good appetite, and a better digestion.

Salad, Mayonnaise.—This is generally considered the king of salads, and it can be made an exceedingly pretty-looking dish. Take two or more French lettuces, clean and dry them as directed above, and take the small heart of one lettuce about the size of a small walnut, uncut from the stalk, so that you can stand it upright in the middle of the salad, raised above the surface. Arrange all the softer parts of the leaves on the top of the salad so as to make as much as possible a smooth surface. Make some Mayonnaise sauce, thick enough to be spread like butter, and mask this little mound and all the surface of the middle of the salad round it with a thin layer of the sauce, so that it looks like the top of a mould of solid custard. Ornament the edge of the salad with hard-boiled eggs cut in quarters, and place between the quarters slices of pickled gherkins and stoned olives. Take a small teaspoonful of French capers, dry them on a cloth, and sprinkle a few of them about an inch apart on the white surface. Next chop up, very finely, about half a teaspoonful of parsley, and see that this doesn't stick together in lumps. Place this on the end of a knife and flip the knife so that the little green specks of parsley fall on the white surface. Next take about half a saltspoonful of finely crumbled bread, and shake these in a saucer with one or two drops of cochineal. This will colour them a bright red, and they will have all the appearance of lobster-coral. Place these red bread-crumbs on the end of a knife and let them fall over the white surface like the parsley. The little red and green specks on the white background make the dish look exceedingly pretty. Before mixing the salad all together add a tablespoonful of tarragon vinegar or lemon-juice.

Tomato Salad.—For making tomato salad you require red, ripe tomatoes; the smoother they are the better, but the chief points are—very ripe and very red. Never use those pink, crinkly tomatoes which look something like milk stained with plum juice. If tomatoes are picked unripe, and then allowed to ripen afterwards, they become rotten and worthless. Slice up half a dozen or more tomatoes—sometimes it will be necessary to remove the core and pips, sometimes not; add a little oil, a little vinegar, and some pepper and salt. Tomato salad is one of the few that are very nice without any oil at all. Of course, this is a matter of taste. Some persons slice up a few onions and add to the tomatoes. In addition to this you can add some slices of cold potatoes. In this latter case, heap the potatoes up in the middle of the dish in the shape of a dome; sprinkle some chopped parsley over the potatoes, put a border of sliced onion round the base, and then a border of sliced tomato outside that. This makes the dish look pretty.

Many persons rub the dish or salad-bowl with a bead of garlic. This is quite sufficient to flavour the salad; but never *chop* garlic for salads.

Egg Salad.—Egg salad consists of an ordinary salad made with French lettuces, with an extra quantity of hard-boiled eggs. If you want to make the salad look very pretty on the top, cut up the lettuces and dress them with oil and vinegar in the ordinary way. Make the tops of the lettuces (which should be placed in a round salad-bowl) as smooth as you can without pressing them down unnecessarily. Now take six hard-boiled eggs, separate the yolks from the whites, powder the yolks, and chop up the whites small. Sprinkle a ring of yellow round the edge of the salad-bowl, say an inch in width, then put a ring of white round, and place the remainder of yolk in the middle, almost up to the centre. Have the centre about two inches in diameter. We now have a yellow centre surrounded by a broad white rim (as, of course, there is more white than yellow), and an outside yellow ring, which meets the white china bowl. Reserve about a teaspoonful of pieces of finely chopped white, and put them in a saucer, with a few drops of cochineal, and shake them. This turns them a bright red. Sprinkle these red specks *very sparingly* on the white, and take about half a teaspoonful of chopped blanched parsley, and sprinkle these green specks on the yellow. This makes the dish look pretty.

German Salad.—German salad is made from cold boiled vegetables chopped up. In Germany, it is made, according to English ideas, from every vegetable you have ever heard of, mixed with a number of vegetables you have never heard of. In England it can be made by chopping up boiled carrot, turnip, cabbage, cauliflower, potato, French beans, Brussels sprouts (whole), celery, raw onion, raw apple, &c. In fact, in making this vegetable salad the motto should be "the more the merrier." In addition to this you will find that they add what is known as *sauer kraut*. This latter is not adapted, as a rule, to English palates. The salad is mixed with oil and vinegar in the ordinary way, the Germans adding much more vinegar than we should care for in this country. The salad is decorated at the finish with boiled beet-root. It is very pretty to cut the beet-root into triangles, the base of the triangle touching the edge of the salad-bowl, the point of the triangle pointing inwards. Cut a star out of a good slice of beet-root, and place it in the centre of the bowl; sprinkle a little chopped blanched parsley over the surface of the mixed vegetables.

Endive Salad.—Endives come into season long before lettuces, and are much used abroad for making salads. The drawback to endive is that it is tough, and the simple remedy is to boil it. Take three or four white-heart endives, throw them into boiling water slightly salted. When they get tender take them out and instantly throw them into cold water, by which means you preserve their colour. When quite cold, take them out again, drain them, dry them thoroughly, and pull them to pieces with the fingers. Now place them in a salad-bowl, keeping the whitest part as much as possible at the top. Place some hard-boiled eggs round the edge, and sprinkle a little chopped blanched parsley over the white endive. You can, if you like, put a few spikes of red beet-root between the quarters of eggs.

It is a great improvement to rub the salad-bowl with a

bead of garlic, or you can rub a crust of bread with a bead of garlic, and toss this lightly about in the salad when you mix it.

Salsify Salad.—Boiled salsify makes a very delicious salad. Take some white salsify, scrape it, and instantly throw it into vinegar and water, by which means you will keep it a pure white. Then, when you have all ready, throw it into boiling water, slightly salted, boil it till it is tender, throw it into cold water, and when cold take it out, drain it and dry it, cut it up into small half-inch pieces (or put it in whole, in sticks, into a salad-bowl), sprinkle a little chopped blanched parsley over the top, dress in the ordinary way with oil and white French vinegar, and be sure to use white pepper, not black. If white wine vinegar is objected to, the juice of a hard fresh lemon is equally good, if not better.

Potato Salad.—Potato salad is generally made from the remains of cold boiled potatoes. Of course, potatoes can be boiled on purpose, in which case they should be allowed to get cold in the water in which they were boiled. New potatoes are far better for the purpose than old. Cut the potatoes into slices, and place them in a salad-bowl with a little finely chopped blanched parsley. You can also add some finely chopped onion or shallot. If you do not add these you can rub the bowl with a bead of garlic. Sprinkle some more chopped parsley over the top of the salad and ornament the edge of the bowl with some thin slices of pickled gherkins. A few stoned olives can also be added. Dress the salad with oil and vinegar in the ordinary way.

Asparagus Salad.—Cold asparagus makes a most delicious salad. It is needless, perhaps, to say it is made from cold boiled asparagus. The best dressing for asparagus salad is somewhat peculiar, and is made as follows:—Take, say, an ounce of butter, put it in a saucer, and melt it in the oven till it is like oil. Now mix in a teaspoonful of made mustard, some pepper, salt, and a dessertspoonful of vinegar. Stir it all together, and as it gets cold it will begin to get thick. Dip all the green part of the asparagus in this, and lay the heads gently, without breaking them, in a vegetable dish, with the white stalk resting on the edge of the dish, and the green part in the middle. Let the salad get perfectly cold, and then serve. Of course, the sauce clings to the asparagus. The asparagus is eaten with the fingers like hot asparagus—a custom now generally recognised.

Artichoke Salad.—This applies to French artichokes, not Jerusalem. In France, artichokes are often served raw for breakfast, on a plate, with a little heap of chopped raw onion and another heap of chopped capers or parsley. The Frenchman mixes a little oil or vinegar on his plate, adding the onion, &c., according to his taste. The leaves are pulled off one by one, the white stalk part dipped in this dressing, and then eaten, by being drawn through the teeth. The artichoke bottom is reserved for the finish as a *bon bouche*, something like a schoolboy who will eat all the pastry round a jam tart, leaving the centre for the *finale*.

Beet-root Salad.—In boiling beet-roots be careful not to break them, or else they will bleed and lose their colour. When the beet-root is boiled and cold, peel it, and cut it into thin slices. It can be dressed with oil and vinegar, or vinegar only, adding pepper and salt. Some persons dress beet-root with a salad-dressing in which cream is used instead of oil; but never use cream *and* oil. To mix cream and oil is like mixing bacon with butter.

Cucumber Salad.—Peel a cucumber and cut it into slices as thin as possible. We might almost add, thinner if possible. Mix it with a little salt, and let it stand, tossing the cucumber about every now and then. By this means you extract all the water from the cucumber. Drain off this water, and add plenty of oil to the cucumber, and then mix it so that every slice comes in contact with the oil. Now add a little pepper, and a very little vinegar, and mix it thoroughly. If you add vinegar to cucumber before the oil some of the slices will taste like sour pickle, as the vinegar soaks into the cucumber. Cucumber should be always served very cold, and is best placed in an ice-chest for an hour before serving. Some people put a piece of ice on the top of the cucumber.

French Bean Salad.—Cold boiled French beans make a very nice salad. A little chopped parsley should be mixed with them, and the salad-bowl can be rubbed with a bead of garlic. Some people soak the beans in vinegar first, and then add oil. This would suit a German palate. A better plan is to add the oil first, with pepper and salt, mix all well together, and then add the vinegar.

Bean Salad.—Cold boiled broad beans make a very nice salad. Rub off the skins so that only the green part is put in the salad-bowl. Rub the bowl with garlic, add a little chopped parsley, then oil, pepper and salt, mix well, and add vinegar last of all.

Haricot Bean Salad.—This can be made from cold, boiled, dried white haricot beans. Add plenty of chopped parsley, rub the bowl with garlic, mix oil, pepper and salt first, vinegar afterwards.

The nicest haricot bean salad is made from the fresh green beans met with abroad. They can be obtained in this country in tins, and a delicious salad can be had at a moment's notice by opening a tin, straining off the liquor, and drying the little green beans, which are very soft and tender, and dressing them with oil and vinegar, in the ordinary way. A little chopped parsley, or garlic flavouring by rubbing the bowl, can be added or not, according to taste.

Celery and Beet-root Salad.—A mixture of celery and beet-root makes a very nice winter salad. The beet-root, of course, is boiled, and the celery generally sliced up thin in a raw state. It is a great improvement to boil the celery till it is *nearly* tender. By this means you improve the salad, and the celery assists in making vegetarian stock.

Water-cress.—Water-cress is sometimes mixed with other salad, but when eaten alone requires no dressing, but only a little salt.

Dandelion Leaf Salad.—Considering that the root of the dandelion is so largely used in medicine for making taraxàcum, it is to be regretted that the leaves of the plant are not utilised in this country as they are abroad for making salad. These leaves can be obtained in London at a few shops in the French colony of Soho. The leaves are washed, dried, placed in a salad-bowl, and dressed with oil and vinegar in the ordinary way.

Cauliflower Salad.—The remains of a cold boiled cauliflower makes a very good salad if only the white part be used. It can be mixed with remains of cold potatoes, some chopped blanched parsley should be sprinkled over the top, and it can be dressed with oil and vinegar in the ordinary way; or it can be served up with a sauce made from oiled butter similar to that described for dressing cold asparagus.

Mustard and Cress.—This is somewhat similar to watercress. When served alone it is generally dipped in salt and eaten with bread-and-butter, but it is very useful to mix with other kinds of salad.

Hop Salad.—In Germany a very nice salad is made from young hops, which are grown very extensively in America and Germany, as English brewers are well aware. The hops are picked when quite young, before they get leafy; they are then boiled till nearly tender. They can be dressed in the English fashion with oil and vinegar, or in the German fashion with vinegar and sugar.

Onion Salad.—Few people are aware of what an excellent salad can be made from the remains of cold boiled Spanish onions. Spanish onions can generally be bought at a penny a pound. They are mild in flavour, very wholesome, and contain a great deal of nourishment. Take a couple of cold boiled Spanish onions, pull them into leaves after they are quite dry, and dress them with a very little oil and vinegar.

Italian Salad.—This is a very delicious salad, met with in Italy. It consists of a great variety of boiled vegetables, which are placed in a mould and served in aspic jelly. This latter, however, is not allowed in vegetarian cookery. A very good imitation, however, can be made as follows :—First take as many cold vegetables as you can, consisting of new potatoes, sliced, and cut up with a cutter into pretty-looking shapes. You can also take green peas, asparagus tops, cold boiled cauliflower, French beans, beet-root, &c. These vegetables should be dressed with a little oil, tarragon vinegar, pepper and salt, and can be placed in a mould or plain round basin. This

SALADS AND SANDWICHES.

basin can now be filled up with a little water thickened with corn-flour, hot. When it is cold, it can be turned out and sent to table in the shape of a mould.

Melon Salad.—Melon is sometimes served abroad as a salad, and a slice of melon is often sent to table at the commencement of dinner, to be eaten with a little salt, cayenne pepper, and sometimes oil and vinegar.

Salads, Sweet.—Apples, oranges, currants, pine-apple, and bananas are sometimes served as salads with syrup and sugar. They make a very nice mixture, or can be served separately. When preserved pine-apples in tins are used for the purpose, the syrup in the tin should be used for dressing the salad. Whole ripe strawberries are a great improvement, as also a wineglassful of brandy and a lump of ice.

Sandwiches.—There is an art in cutting sandwiches—a fact which persons in the habit of frequenting railway restaurants will hardly realise. A tinned loaf is best for the purpose if we wish to avoid waste. The great thing is to have the two slices of bread to fit together neatly, and there is no occasion to cut off the crusts when made from a well-rasped tin loaf. First cut off the crust from the top of the loaf, which, of course, must be used for some other purpose. The best use for this top slice is to toast it lightly on the crumby side, and cut it up into little pieces to be served with soup. Next take the loaf, cut off one thin slice, evenly, and let it fall on its back on the board you are using. Now butter very slightly the upper surface. Next butter the top of the loaf, cut another thin slice, and, of course, these two pieces of bread will be perfectly level, and, if the two buttered sides be placed together, will fit round the edge exactly.

Tomato Sandwiches.—Cut some very ripe red tomatoes into thin slices, and cut them parallel with the core, as otherwise you will get them in rings from which the core will drop out. Sprinkle some thin slices of bread-and-butter with mustard and cress, dip the slices of tomato into a dressing made with a little oil, pepper, and salt, well mixed up. Put these between the bread-and-butter, and cut them into squares or triangles with a very sharp knife. These sandwiches are very cool and refreshing, and make a most agreeable supper after a hot and crowded ball-room. If you wish to have them look pretty, pile them up in the centre of a silver dish, and place a few ripe red tomatoes round the base on some bright green parsley. Place the dish in an ice-chest for an hour before it is eaten.

Mustard and Cress Sandwiches.—Place well-washed and dried mustard and cress between two slices of bread-and-butter, and trim the edges. It is best to pepper and salt the bread-and-butter first. Pile up the sandwiches on a silver dish, and sprinkle some loose mustard and cress round the base.

Egg Sandwiches.—Cut some hard-boiled eggs into very thin slices; season them with pepper and salt, and place them between two slices of thin bread-and-butter; cut the sandwiches into triangles or squares, pile them up in a silver dish, place plenty of fresh green parsley round the base of the dish, and place some hard-boiled eggs, cut in halves, on the parsley, which will show what the sandwiches are composed of.

Indian Sandwiches.—These are exactly similar to the above, with the addition that the slices of hard-boiled eggs are seasoned with a little curry-powder. If hard-boiled eggs in halves are placed round the base of the dish, each half-egg should be sprinkled with curry-powder in order to show what the sandwiches are.

Mushroom Sandwiches.—Take a pint of fresh button mushrooms, peel them, and throw them into lemon-juice and water, in order to preserve their colour; or else take the contents of a tin of mushrooms, chop them up and stew them in a frying-pan very gently with a little butter, pepper, salt, a pinch of thyme, and the juice of a whole lemon to every pint of mushrooms. When tender, rub the mixture through a wire sieve while the butter is warm and the mixture moist. Add a teaspoonful of finely chopped blanched parsley, spread this mixture while still warm on a thin slice of bread, and cover it over with another thin slice of bread, and press the two slices of bread together. When the mixture gets quite cold, the butter will set and the sandwiches get quite firm.

The bread need not be buttered, as the mixture contains butter enough. Pile these sandwiches up on a silver dish, surround the dish with plenty of fresh parsley, and place a few fresh mushrooms whole, stalk and all, round them, as if they are growing out of the parsley.

Cheese Sandwiches.—Oil a little butter, add some pepper and salt, and a spoonful of made mustard and a pinch of cayenne pepper. When this mixture is nearly cold, use it for buttering some thin slices of bread, and, before it is quite cold, sprinkle them with some grated Parmesan cheese. Put the two slices of bread together and press them, and, when cold, cut them into squares or triangles. Place plenty of fresh green parsley round the dish, and, if you are using hard-boiled eggs for other purposes, take the end of the white of egg, which has a little cup in it not much bigger than the top of the finger, and put a little heap of Parmesan cheese in each cup. Place a few of these round the base of the dish, on the parsley, in order to show what the sandwiches are composed of.

Cream-Cheese Sandwiches.—Chop up some of the white part of a head of celery very fine, and pound it in a mortar with a little butter; season it with some salt. Use this mixture and butter some thin slices of bread, place a thin slice of cream cheese between these slices, cut the sandwiches into squares or triangles with a very sharp knife, and pile the sandwiches up on a silver dish. Surround the dish with parsley, and place a few slices of cream-cheese, cut round the size of a halfpenny, round the base, stick a little piece of the yellowish-white leaves of the heart of celery in each piece.

CHAPTER VI.

SAVOURY DISHES.

MUSHROOMS.

In many parts of the country mushrooms grow so plentifully that their cost may be considered almost nothing. On the other hand, if they have to be bought fresh, at certain seasons of the year they are very expensive, while tinned mushrooms, which can always be depended upon, cannot be regarded in any other light than that of a luxury.

When mushrooms can be gathered in the fields like blackberries they are a great boon to vegetarians. Of course, great care must be taken that only genuine mushrooms are picked, as there have been some terrible instances of poisoning from fungi being gathered by mistake, as many Cockney tourists know to their cost. As a rule, in England all mushrooms bought in markets can be depended upon. In France, where mushrooms are very plentiful, an inspector is appointed in every market, and no mushrooms are allowed to be sold unless they have first received his sanction. This is a wise precaution in the right direction.

One important word of warning before leaving the subject. Mushrooms should be eaten *freshly gathered*, and, if allowed to get stale, those which were perfectly wholesome when fresh picked become absolutely poisonous. The symptoms are somewhat similar to narcotic poisoning. This particularly applies to the larger and coarser kind that give out black juice.

Mushrooms, Plain, Grilled.—The larger kinds of mushrooms are best for the purpose. The flat mushrooms should be washed, dried, and peeled. They are then cooked slowly over a clear fire, and a small wire gridiron, like those sold at a penny or twopence each, is better adapted for the purpose than the ordinary gridiron used for grilling steak. The gridiron should be kept high above the fire. The mushrooms should be dipped in oil, or oiled butter, and care should be taken that they do not stick to the bars. They should be served very hot, with pepper and salt and a squeeze of lemon-juice.

Mushrooms, Fried.—When mushrooms are very small they are more easily fried than grilled. They should be washed, dried and peeled, placed in a frying-pan, with a little butter, pepper and salt, and cooked till tender. They are very nice served on toast, and the butter in which they are cooked can be poured on the toast first, and the mushrooms arranged on the top afterwards. A squeeze of lemon-juice is an improvement.

Mushrooms au gratin.—This is a very delicious dish, and is often served as an entrée at first-class dinners. They are made from what are known as cup mushrooms. It is best to pick mushrooms, as far as possible, the same size, the cup being about two inches in diameter. Peel the mushrooms very carefully, without breaking them, cut out the stalks close down with a spoon, scoop out the inside of the cup, so as to make it hollow. Now peel the stalks and chop them up with all the scooped part of the mushroom, with, supposing we are making ten cups, a piece of onion as big as the top of the thumb down to the first joint. To this add a brimming teaspoonful of chopped parsley, or even a little more, a saltspoonful of dried thyme, or half this quantity of fresh thyme. Fry all this in a frying-pan, in a little butter. The aroma is delicious. Then add sufficient dried bread-crumbs that have been rubbed through a wire sieve to make the whole into a moist paste, fill each of the cups with this mixture so that the top is as convex as the cup of the mushroom, having first seasoned the mixture with a little pepper, salt, and lemon-juice. Shake some fine bread-raspings over the top so as to make them of a nice golden-brown colour, pour a little drop of oil into a baking-tin, place the mushrooms in it, and bake them gently in an oven till the cup part of the mushroom becomes soft and tender, but take care they do not cook till they break. Now take them out carefully with an egg-slice, and place them on a dish—a silver dish is best for the purpose—and place some nice, crisp, fried parsley round the edge.

VEGETARIAN COOKERY.

Mushrooms à la Bordelaise.—This, as the name implies, is a French recipe. It consists of ordinary grilled mushrooms, served in a sauce composed of oil or oiled butter, chopped up with parsley and garlic, thickened with the yolks of eggs.

Mushrooms à la Provençale.—This is an Italian recipe. You must first wash, peel, and dry the mushrooms, and then soak them for some time in what is called a *marinade*, which is another word for pickle, of oil mixed with chopped garlic, pepper, and salt. They are then stewed in oil with plenty of chopped parsley over rather a brisk fire. Squeeze a little lemon-juice over them and serve them in a dish surrounded with a little fried or toasted bread.

Mushroom Forcemeat.—The mushrooms after being cleaned should be chopped up and fried in a little butter; lemon-juice should be added before they are chopped in order to preserve their colour. One or two hard-boiled yolks of eggs can be added to the mixture, and the whole rubbed through a wire sieve while hot. When the mixture is hot it should be moist, but, of course, when it gets cold, owing to the butter it will be hard. This mushroom forcemeat can be used for a variety of purposes.

Mushroom Pie.—Wash, dry, and peel some mushrooms, and cut them into slices with an equal quantity of cut-up potatoes. Bake these in a pie, having first moistened the potatoes and mushrooms in a little butter. Add pepper and salt and a small pinch of thyme. Cover them with a little water and put some paste over the dish in the ordinary way. It is a great improvement, after the pie is baked, to pour in some essence of mushrooms made from stewing the stalks and peelings in a little water. A single onion should be put in with them.

Mushroom Pie, Cold.—Prepare the mushrooms, potatoes, and essence of mushroom as directed above, adding a little chopped parsley. Bake all these in the dish before you cover with paste, add also an extra seasoning of pepper. When the mushrooms and potatoes are perfectly tender, strain off all the juice or gravy, and thicken it with corn-flour; put this back in the pie-dish and mix all well together, and pile it up in the middle of the dish so that the centre is raised above the edge. Let this get quite cold, then cover it with puff-paste, and as soon as the pastry is done take it out of the oven and let the pie get cold. This can now be cut in slices.

Mushroom Pudding.—Make a mixture of mushrooms, potatoes, &c., exactly similar to that for making a pie. Place this in a basin with only sufficient water to moisten the ingredients, cover the basin with bread-crumbs soaked in milk, and steam the basin in the ordinary way.

Tomatoes, Grilled.—What is necessary is a clear fire and a gridiron in which the bars are not too far apart. The disputed point is, should the tomatoes be grilled whole or cut in half? This may be considered a matter of taste, but personally we prefer them grilled whole. Moisten the tomato in a little oil or oiled butter, and grill them carefully, as they are apt to break. Grilled tomatoes are very nice with plain boiled macaroni, or can be served up on boiled rice.

Tomatoes, Baked.—Place the tomatoes in a tin with a little butter, and occasionally baste them with the butter. When they are tender, they can be served either plain or with boiled macaroni or rice. The butter and juice in the tin should be poured over them.

Tomatoes, Fried.—Place the tomatoes in a frying-pan with a little butter, and fry them until they are tender. Pour the contents of the frying-pan over them, serve plain, or with macaroni or rice.

Tomatoes, Stewed.—Take half a dozen good-sized tomatoes, and chop up very finely one onion about the same size as the tomatoes. Moisten the bottom of a stew-pan with a little butter, and sprinkle the chopped onion over the tomatoes. Add a dessertspoonful of water; place the lid on the stewpan, which ought to fit tightly. It is best to put a weight on the lid of the stew-pan, such as a flat-iron. Place the stew-pan on the fire, and let them steam till they are tender. They are cooked this way in Spain and Portugal, and very often chopped garlic is used instead of onion.

Tomatoes au gratin.—Take a dozen ripe tomatoes, cut off the stalks, and squeeze out the juice and pips. Next take a few mushrooms and make a mixture exactly similar to that which was used to fill the inside of Mushrooms au gratin. Fill each tomato with some of this mixture, so that it assumes its original shape and tight skin. The top or hole where the stalk was cut out will probably be about the size of a shilling or halfpenny. Shake some bright-coloured bread raspings over this spot without letting them fall on the red tomato. In order to do this, cut a round hole the right size in a stiff piece of paper. Place the tomatoes in a stew-pan or a baking-dish in the oven, moistened with a little oil. The oil should be about the eighth of an inch deep. Stew or bake the tomatoes till they are tender, and then take them out carefully with an egg-slice, and serve them surrounded with fried parsley. If placed in a silver dish this has a very pretty appearance.

Tomato Pie.—Slice up an equal number of ripe tomatoes and potatoes. Place them in a pie-dish with enough oiled butter to moisten them. Add a brimming teaspoonful of chopped parsley, a pinch of thyme, pepper, and salt, and, if possible, a few peeled mushrooms, which will be found to be a very great improvement. Cover the pie with paste, and bake in the oven.

Tomato Pie (another way).—Proceed as in making an ordinary potato pie. Add a small bottle of tomato conserve, cover with paste, and bake in the ordinary way.

Potato Pie.—Peel and slice up some potatoes as thin as possible. At the same time slice up some onions. If Spanish onions are used allow equal quantities of potatoes and onions, but if ordinary onions are used allow only half this quantity. Place a layer of sliced onion and sliced potato alternately. Add some pepper, salt, and sufficient butter to moisten the potato and butter before any water is added. Pour in some water and add a teaspoonful of chopped parsley, cover the pie with paste, and bake in the ordinary way.

Potato Pie (another way).—Butter a shallow pie-dish rather thickly. Line the edges with a good crust, and then fill the pie with mashed potatoes seasoned with pepper, salt, and grated nutmeg. Lay over them some small lumps of butter, hard-boiled eggs, blanched almonds, sliced dates, sliced lemon and candied peel. Cover the dish with pastry and bake the pie in a well-heated oven for half an hour or more, according to the size of the pie.

Pumpkin Pie.—Peel a ripe pumpkin and chip off the rind or skin, halve it, and take out the seed and fluffy part in the centre, which throw away. Cut the pumpkin into small, thin slices, fill a pie-dish therewith, add to it half a teaspoonful of all spice and a tablespoonful of sugar, with a small quantity of water. Cover with a nice light paste and bake in the ordinary way. Pumpkin pie is greatly improved by being eaten with Devonshire cream and sugar. An equal quantity of apples with the pumpkin will make a still more delicious pie.

Pumpkin Pudding.—Take a large pumpkin, pare it, and remove the seeds. Cut half of it into thin slices, and boil these gently in water until they are quite soft, then rub them through a fine sieve with the back of a wooden spoon. Measure the pulp, and with each pint put four ounces of butter and a large nutmeg, grated. Stir the mixture briskly for a minute or two, then add the third of a pint of hot milk and four well-beaten eggs. Pour the pudding into a buttered dish, and bake in a moderate oven for about an hour. Sugar may be added to taste.

Potato Cheesecake.—(*See* CHEESECAKES.)

Cheese with Fried Bread.—Take some stale bread, and cut it into strips about three inches long and one wide and one inch thick. Fry the bread in some butter or oil till it is a nice bright golden colour. Spread a layer of made mustard over the strips of fried bread, and then cover them with grated Parmesan cheese, pile them up on a dish, and place them in the oven. As soon as the cheese begins to melt serve them very hot.

Cheese, Savoury.—Take equal quantities of grated Parmesan cheese, butter, and flour; add a little salt and cayenne pepper, make these into a paste with some water, roll out the paste thin till it is about a quarter of an inch thick; cut it into strips and bake them in the oven till they are a nice brown, and serve hot.

Cheese Soufflé.—(*See* OMELETS.)

Cheese Pudding.—Mix half a pound of grated Parmesan cheese with four eggs, well beaten up; mix in also two ounces of butter, which should be first beaten to a cream, add half a pint of milk and pour the mixture into a well-buttered pie-dish, sprinkle some grated Parmesan cheese over the top, and bake in the oven for about half an hour. The pudding will be lighter if two of the whites of eggs are beaten to a stiff froth. The edge of the pie-dish can be lined with puff-paste.

Cheese Ramequins.—Put half a pound of grated Parmesan cheese in a stew-pan with a quarter of a pound of butter and a quarter of a pint of water; add a little pepper and salt, and as much flour as will make the whole into a thick paste. Mix up with the paste as many well-beaten-up eggs as will make the paste not too liquid to be moulded into a shape. The eggs should be beaten till they froth. Now, with a tablespoon, mould this mixture into shapes like a meringue or egg; place these on a buttered tin and bake them till they are a nice brown colour.

Cheese, Stewed.—When the remains of cheese have got very dry it is a good plan to use it up in the shape of stewed cheese. Break up the cheese and put it in a small stew-pan with about a quarter its weight of butter; add a little milk, and let the cheese stew gently till it is dissolved. At the finish, and when you have removed it from the fire, add a well-beaten-up egg. This can be served on toast, or it can be poured on to a dish and pieces of toasted bread stuck in it.

Cheese Straws.—Mix equal quantities of grated Parmesan cheese, grated bread-crumbs that have been rubbed through a wire sieve, butter, and flour; add a little cayenne and grated nutmeg. Make it into a thick paste, roll it out very thin, cut it into strips, and bake for a few minutes in a fierce oven.

Cheese, Toasted.—This is best done in a Dutch oven, so that when one side is toasted you can turn the oven and toast the back; as soon as the cheese begins to melt it is done. As it gets cold very quickly, and when cold gets hard, it is best served on hot-water plates.

Cheese, Devilled.—Chop up some hot pickles, add some

SAVOURY DISHES.

cayenne pepper and mustard. Melt some cheese in a stew-pan with a little butter, mix in the pickles, and serve on toast.

Welsh Rarebit.—Toast a large slice of bread; in the meantime melt some cheese in the saucepan with a little butter. When the cheese is melted it will be found that a good deal of oiled butter floats on the top. Pour this over the dry toast first, and then pour the melted cheese afterwards. Some persons add a teaspoonful of Worcester sauce to the cheese, and others a tablespoonful of good old Burton ale over the top.

Ayoli.—This is a dish almost peculiar to the South of France. Soak some crusts of bread in water, squeeze them dry, and add two cloves of garlic chopped fine, six blanched almonds, also chopped very fine, and a yolk of an egg; mix up the whole into a smooth paste with a little oil.

Pumpkin à la Parmesane.—Cut a large pumpkin into square pieces and boil them for about a quarter of an hour in salt and water, and take them out, drain them, and put them in a stew-pan with a little butter, salt, and grated nutmeg; fry them, sprinkle them with a little Parmesan cheese, and bake them for a short time in the oven till the cheese begins to melt, and then serve. This is an Italian recipe.

Zucchetti farcis.—Take some very small gourds or pumpkins, boil them for about a quarter of an hour in salt and water, and then fill them with a forcemeat made as follows: Take some crumb of bread and soak it in milk, squeeze it and add the yolks of two hard-boiled eggs and two raw yolks; chop up very finely half a dozen blanched almonds with a couple of cloves; add two ounces of grated Parmesan cheese, and a little salt and grated nutmeg. Stew these gourds in butter and serve them with white sauce.

Stuffed Onions (Italian fashion).—Parboil some large onions, stamp out the core after they have been allowed to get quite cold in a little water; fill the inside with forcemeat similar to the above; fry them, squeeze the juice of a lemon over them, with a little pepper.

Polenta.—Polenta is made from ground Indian corn, and is seen in Italian shop-windows in the form of a yellow powder;

it is made into a paste with boiling water, sprinkled with Parmesan cheese, and baked in the oven.

Piroski Sernikis.—This dish is met with in Poland, and is made by mixing up two pounds of cream-cheese, three-quarters of a pound of fine bread-crumbs that have been rubbed through a wire sieve, six eggs well beaten up; add a little cream or milk, four ounces of washed grocer's currants, one ounce of sugar, half a grated nutmeg; and when the whole is thoroughly mixed add as much flour as is necessary to make the whole into a paste that can be rolled into balls. These balls should not be much bigger than a walnut. Flour them, and then flatten them into little cakes and fry them a nice brown in some butter.

Of course, a smaller quantity can be made by using these ingredients in proportion.

Nalesnikis (Polish Pancakes).—Take eight eggs and beat them up very thoroughly with about a pint and a half of milk, or still better, cream, two ounces of butter that has been oiled, half a grated nutmeg, and about a dozen lumps of sugar that have been rubbed on the outside of a lemon; mix in sufficient flour—about three-quarters of a pound will be required—to make the whole into a very smooth batter. Melt a little butter in a frying-pan, pour it all over the pan, and when it frizzles, pour in some of the batter, and sprinkle over a few currants; when the pancake is fried, shake some powdered sugar over it, roll it up like an ordinary pancake, and serve hot.

FRITTERS.

Batter for Savoury Fritters.—Put six ounces of flour into a basin, with a pinch of salt, the yolk of one egg, and a quarter of a pint of warm water. Work this round and round with a wooden spoon till it is perfectly smooth and looks like thick cream. About half an hour before the batter is wanted for use whip the white of one egg to a stiff froth and mix it lightly in.

Mushroom Fritters.—Make some mushroom forcemeat; let it get quite cold on a dish about a quarter of an inch thick. Cut out some small rounds, about the size of a penny-piece.

They fry better if slightly oval. Have ready some thick batter (*See* BATTER). Have also ready in a saucepan some boiling oil, which should be heated to about 350°. Place a frying-basket in the saucepan, flour the rounds of mushroom forcemeat so as to make them perfectly dry on the outside. Dip these pieces into the batter and throw them into the boiling oil. The great heat of the oil will set the batter before the mushroom forcemeat has time to melt. Directly the batter is a nice light-brown colour, lift them out of the boiling oil with the frying-basket, and throw them on to a cloth to drain. Break off the outside pieces of batter, and serve the fritters on a neatly folded napkin on a dish surrounded by fried parsley.

The beauty of these fritters is that when they are eaten the inside is moist, owing, of course, to the heat having melted the forcemeat.

Tomato Fritters.—Make some mushroom forcemeat and spread it out as thin as possible. Take some ripe tomatoes, cut them in slices, dip the slice in vinegar, drain it and pepper it, and then wrap this thin slice of tomato in a layer of mushroom forcemeat. Bring the edges together, flour it, dip it into batter (*see* BATTER), and throw it into boiling oil as in making mushroom fritters (*see* MUSHROOM FRITTERS).

Imitation Game Fritters.—Make some mushroom forcemeat as directed under the heading "Mushroom Forcemeat," with the addition of, when you fry the mushrooms, chop up and fry with them two heads of garlic, and add a saltspoonful of aromatic flavouring herbs. (These are sold in bottles by all grocers under the name of "Herbaceous Mixture.") Then proceed exactly as if you were making mushroom fritters (*see* MUSHROOM FRITTERS).

Hominy Fritters.—These are made from remains of cold boiled hominy, cut in thin slices, which must be dipped in batter and fried in boiling oil.

Cheese Fritters.—Pound some dry cheese, or take about three ounces of Parmesan cheese, and mix it with a few bread-crumbs, a piece of butter, a pinch of cayenne pepper, and the yolk of an egg, till the whole becomes a thick paste. Roll the mixture into very small balls, flatten them, flour them, dip them into batter, and throw them into boiling oil in the ordinary way. Put them in the oven for five minutes before serving them.

Sage and Onion Fritters.—Make some ordinary sage and onion stuffing, allowing one fresh sage leaf or two dried to each parboiled onion; add pepper and salt and dried breadcrumbs. Now moisten the whole with clarified butter, till the mixture becomes a moist pulp. When it begins to get cold and sets, roll it into small balls, the size of a very small walnut, flatten these and let them get quite cold, then flour them, dip them into batter, and throw them into boiling oil; remove them with the frying-basket, and serve with fried parsley.

Spinach Fritters.—Make a little thick purée of spinach, add a pinch of savoury herbs containing marjoram; mix in a little clarified butter and one or two lumps of sugar rubbed on the outside of a lemon, as well as a little grated nutmeg. Roll the mixture into very small balls, or else they will break, flatten them, flour them, dip them into batter, and throw them into boiling oil, and serve immediately.

Fritters, Sweet.—In making sweet fritters, the same kind of batter will do as we used for making savoury fritters, though many cooks add a little powdered sugar. The same principles hold good. The oil must be heated to a temperature of 350°, and a frying-basket must be used. Instead of flouring the substances employed to make them dry, before being dipped into the batter, which is an essential point in making fritters, we must use finely powdered sugar, and it will be found a saving of both time and trouble to buy pounded sugar for the purpose. It is sold by grocers under the name of castor sugar. We cannot make this at home in a pestle and mortar to the same degree of fineness any more than we could grind our own flour. We cannot compete with machinery.

Apple Fritters.—Peel some apples, cut them in slices across the core, and stamp out the core. It is customary, where wine, &c., is not objected to, to soak these rings of apples for several hours in a mixture of brandy, grated lemon or orange peel and sugar, or better still, to rub some lumps of sugar on the outside of a lemon or orange and dissolve this in the brandy. Of course, brandy is not necessary, but the custom is worth mentioning. The rings of apple can be soaked for some time in syrup flavoured this way. They must then be made dry by being dipped in powdered sugar, then dipped into batter and thrown, one at a time, into a saucepan containing smoking hot oil in which a wire frying-basket has been placed. Directly the fritters are a nice brown, take them out, break off the rough pieces, shake some finely powdered sugar over them, pile them up on a dish, and serve.

Apricot Fritters.—These can be made from fresh apricots or tinned ones, not too ripe; if they break they are not fitted. When made from fresh apricots they should be peeled, cut in halves, the round end removed, dipped in powdered sugar, then dipped in batter, thrown into boiling oil, and finished like apple fritters. Some persons soak the apricots in brandy.

Banana Fritters.—Banana fritters can be made from the bananas as sold in this country, and it is a mistake to think that when they are black outside they are bad. When in this state they are sometimes sold as cheap as six a penny. Peel the bananas, cut them into slices half an inch thick, dip them into finely powdered sugar and then into batter, and finish as directed in apple fritters.

Some persons soak the slices of banana in maraschino.

Custard Fritters.—Take half a pint of cream in which some cinnamon and lemon have been boiled, add to this five yolks of eggs, a little flour, and about three ounces of sugar. Put this into a pie-dish, well buttered, and steam it till the custard becomes quite set; then let it get cold, and cut it into slices about half an inch thick and an inch and a half long, sprinkle each piece with a little powdered cinnamon, and make it quite dry with some powdered sugar. Then dip each piece into batter, throw them one by one into boiling oil, and finish as directed for apple fritters.

Almond Fritters, Chocolate Fritters, Coffee Fritters, Vanilla Fritters, &c.—These fritters are made exactly in the same way as custard fritters, only substituting powdered chocolate, pounded almonds, essence of coffee, or essence of vanilla, for the powdered cinnamon.

Frangipane Fritters.—Make a Frangipane cream by mixing eggs with a little cold potato, butter, sugar, and powdered ratafias, the proportion being a quarter of a pound of butter, four eggs, six ounces of sugar, one cold floury potato, and a quarter of a pound of ratafias. Bake or steam this until it is set, and proceed as in custard fritters. Many persons add the flavouring of a little rum.

Peach Fritters.—These are made exactly similar to apricot fritters, bearing in mind that if they are made from tinned peaches only the firm pieces, and not pulpy ones, must be used for the purpose. Proceed exactly as directed for apricot fritters.

If any liqueur is used, noyeau is best adapted for the purpose.

Potato Fritters.—Mix up some floury potato with a quarter of a pound of butter, a well-beaten-up egg, and three ounces of sugar, some of which has been rubbed on the outside of a lemon. The addition of a little cream is a great improvement. Roll the mixture into small balls and flour them; they are then fried just as they are, without being dipped into batter.

Pine-apple Fritters.—These can be made from fresh pine-apples or tinned. They should be cut into slices like apple fritters if the pine-apple is small, but if the pine-apple is large they can be cut into strips three inches long and one wide and half an inch thick. These must be dipped in powdered sugar, then into batter, and finished as directed for apple fritters.

If any liqueur is used, maraschino is best adapted to the purpose.

Orange Fritters.—Only first-class oranges are adapted for this purpose. Thick-skinned and woolly oranges are no use. Peel a thin-skinned ripe orange, divide each orange into about six pieces, soak these in a syrup flavoured with sugar rubbed on the outside of an orange, and if liqueur is used make the syrup with brandy. After they have soaked some time, remove any pips, dip each piece into batter, and proceed as directed for apple fritters.

Cream Fritters.—Rub some lumps of sugar on the outside of an orange, pound them, and mix with a little cream; take some small pieces of stale white cake, such as Madeira cake or what the French call brioche. Soak these pieces of stale cake, which must be cut small and thin, or they will break, in the orange-flavoured cream, dry each piece in some finely-powdered sugar, dip it into batter, and proceed as directed for making apple fritters.

German Fritters.—Take some small stale pieces of cake, and soak them in a little milk or cream flavoured with essence of vanilla and sweetened with a little sugar. Take them out, and let them get a little dry on the outside, then dip them in a well-beaten-up egg, cover them with bread-crumbs, and fry a nice golden-brown colour.

Rice and Ginger Fritters.—Boil a small quantity of rice in milk and add some preserved ginger chopped small, some sugar, and one or more eggs, sufficient to set the mixture when baked in a pie-dish. Bake till set, then cut into slices about two inches long, an inch wide, and half an inch thick; dry these pieces with powdered sugar, dip into batter, and finish as directed for making apple fritters.

Rice Fritters.—A variety of fritters could be made from a small baked rice pudding, flavoured with various kinds of essences, spices, orange marmalade, peach marmalade, fresh lime marmalade, apricot jam, &c., proceeding exactly as directed above.

E *

CHAPTER VII.

VEGETABLES.

SUBSTANTIAL VEGETABLES.

VEGETABLES may be roughly divided into two classes—those that may be called substantial and which are adapted to form a meal in themselves, and those of a lighter kind, which cannot be said to make a sufficient repast unless eaten with bread.

Potatoes were first introduced into this country about 400 years ago, tobacco being introduced about the same period, and we cannot disguise the fact that there are many who regard the latter as the greater blessing of the two. If Sir Henry Thompson is right in stating that tobacco is the great ally of temperance, there may be some ground for this opinion.

Potatoes form an important article of food for the body, while, whatever effect tobacco may have upon the thinking powers of mankind, it is almost the only product of the vegetable kingdom that is absolutely uneatable even when placed within the reach of those in the last stage of starvation.

In some parts, especially in Ireland, potatoes form almost the only food of the population, just as rice does in hotter climates, and when the crop fails famine ensues. When potatoes form the only kind of food, a very large quantity has to be eaten by a hard-working man in order for him to receive sufficient nourishment to keep his body healthy, the amount required being not less than ten pounds per day. If, on the other hand, a certain amount of fat or oil of some kind be mixed with them, a far less quantity will suffice. Hence we find in Ireland that, wherever it is possible, either some kind of oily fish, such as herring, is taken with them, or, which is much more to the point with vegetarians, a certain quantity of fat is obtained in the shape of milk.

It must also be remembered that four pounds of raw potatoes contain only one pound of solid food, the remaining three pounds being water. It is important, for those who first commence a vegetarian diet, to remember that vegetables like peas, haricot beans, and lentils are far superior to potatoes so far as nourishment is concerned, for many are apt to jump to the conclusion that potatoes are the very best substitute for bread and milk. So, too, is oatmeal. A Scotchman requires a far less quantity of oatmeal to sustain life than an Irishman does potatoes; hence it is a very important point to remember that, if we depend upon potatoes to any great extent for our daily food, we should cook them in such a manner as to entail as little waste as possible. We will now try and explain, as briefly as possible, the best method of serving.

Potatoes, Plain Boiled.—The best method of having potatoes, if we wish to study economy, is to boil them in their jackets, as it is generally admitted that the most nourishing part is that which lies nearest to the skin. There are many houses in the country where an inexperienced cook will peel, say four pounds of potatoes, and throw the peel into the pig-tub, where the pig gets a better meal than the family.

When potatoes are boiled in their skins, they should be thoroughly washed and scrubbed with a hard brush. Old potatoes should be put into cold water, and when the water boils the time should a good deal depend upon the size of the potatoes. When the potatoes are large, the chief principle to be borne in mind is, do not let them boil too quickly or cook too quickly. We must avoid having the outside pulpy while the inside is hard. The water, which should be slightly salted, should more than cover them, and, if the potatoes are very large, directly the water comes to the boil it is a good plan to throw in a little cold water to take it off the boil. It is quite impossible to lay down any exact law in regard to boiling potatoes. We cannot do more than give general principles which can only be carried out by cooks who possess a little common sense.

Small new potatoes are an extreme in one direction. They should be thrown into boiling water, and are generally cooked in about ten minutes or a quarter of an hour. Large old potatoes should be put into cold water and, as we have stated, the water should not be allowed to boil too soon, and it will take very often an hour to boil them properly. Between these two extremes there is a gradually ascending scale which must be left to the judgment of the cook. It is as impossible to lay down any hard-and-fast line with regard to time in boiling potatoes as it would be to say at what exact point in the thermometer between freezing and 80° in the shade a man should put on his top coat.

If we may be allowed the expression, "old new" potatoes should be thrown into neither boiling water nor cold water, but lukewarm water. Again, in boiling potatoes, especially in the case of old ones, some little allowance must be made for the time of year. In winter, they require longer time, and we may here mention the fact that it is very important that potatoes, after they are dug, should not be left out of doors and exposed to a hard frost, as in this case a chemical change takes place in which the starch is converted into sugar.

When potatoes are boiled in their jackets sufficiently, which fact is generally tested by sticking a steel fork into them, they should be strained off, and allowed to get dry for a few minutes in the saucepan, which should be removed from the fire, as at times the potatoes are apt to stick and burn.

When large potatoes are peeled before they are boiled, we should endeavour to send them to table floury, and this is often said to be the test of a really good cook. After the water has been strained off from the potatoes, a dry cloth should be placed under the lid of the saucepan, and the lid should only be placed half on, *i.e.*, it should not be fitted down tight. It is also as well to give the saucepan now and then a shake, but do not overdo the shaking and break them. About five or ten minutes is generally sufficient.

Potatoes, Steamed.—Potatoes can be steamed in their jackets, and it is a more economical method than peeling. It should be remembered, however, that steam is hotter than boiling water. If plain water is underneath and boils furiously, and the steam is well shut in, they will cook very quickly; but if, as is generally the case, something else is in the saucepan under the steamer, boiling gently, this does not apply. We refer to the ordinary steamer met with in private houses, and not to the ones used in the large hotels and restaurants.

Potatoes, Baked.—When potatoes are baked in the oven in their jackets the larger they are the better. The oven must not be too fierce, and ample time should be allowed. Baked potatoes require quite two hours. This only refers to those baked in their jackets. When potatoes are cut up and baked in a tin they require some kind of fat, which, of course, in vegetarian cookery must be either oil or butter.

Potatoes, Mashed.—What may be termed high-class mashed potatoes are made by mashing up ordinary boiled potatoes with a little milk *previously boiled*, a little butter, and passing the whole through a wire sieve, when a little cream, butter and salt is added.

In private houses mashed potatoes are generally made from the remains of cold boiled potatoes, or when the cook, in boiling the potatoes, has made a failure. Still, of course, potatoes are boiled often expressly for the purpose of being mashed. This is often the case where old potatoes have to be cut into all sorts of shapes and sizes in order to get rid of the black spots. As soon as the potatoes are boiled they are generally moistened in the saucepan with a little drop of milk. It is undoubtedly an improvement, and also entails very little extra trouble, to boil the milk first. There is a difference in flavour, which is very marked, between milk that has been boiled and raw milk. Suppose you have coffee for breakfast, add boiling milk to one cup and raw milk to another, and then see how great a difference there will be in the flavour of the two. A little butter should be added to mashed potatoes, but it is not really essential. Mashed potatoes can be served in the shape of a mould, that is, they can be shaped in a mould and then browned in the oven. If you serve mashed potatoes in an ordinary dish, and pile them up in the shape of a dome, the dish will look much prettier if you score it round with a fork and then place the dish in a fairly fierce oven; the edges will brown, but be careful that they don't get burnt black.

Potatoes, Fried.—The best lesson, if you wish to fry potatoes nicely, is to look in at the window of a fried fish shop, where every condition is fulfilled that is likely to lead to perfection. The bath of oil is deep and smoking hot, and in sufficient quantity not to lose greatly in temperature on the introduction of the frying-basket containing the potatoes. The potatoes must be cut up into small pieces, not much bigger in thickness than the little finger; these are plunged into the smoking hot oil, and as soon as they are *slightly* browned on the outside they are done. They acquire a darker colour after they are removed from the oil, and the inside will go on cooking for several minutes. It would be quite impossible to eat fried potatoes directly they are taken out of the fat, as they would burn the mouth terribly. It is best to throw the fried potatoes into a cloth for a few seconds.

Potato Chips.—Potato chips are ordinary fried potatoes cut up when raw into little pieces about the size and thickness of a lucifer match. They, of course, will cook very quickly. They should be removed from the oil directly they *begin* to turn colour.

Potato Ribbon.—Potato ribbon is simply ordinary fried potatoes, in which the raw potato is cut in the shape of a ribbon. You take a potato and peel it in the ordinary way. You then take this and, with not too sharp a knife, peel it like an apple, making the strip as long as you can, like children sometimes do when they throw the apple peel over their shoulders to see what letter it will make. You can go on peeling the potato round and round till there is none left. These ribbons are thrown into boiling oil, and must be removed as soon as they begin to turn colour. When piled up in a dish they look very pretty, and with a little pepper and salt, and a squeeze of lemon-juice, make an excellent meal when eaten with bread.

Potato Sauté.—This dish is more frequently met with abroad than in England, except in foreign restaurants. It is made by taking the remains of ordinary plain-boiled potatoes that are not floury. These are cut up into small pieces about the size of the thumb, no particular shape being necessary. They are thrown into a frying-pan with a little butter, and fried gently till the edges begin to brown; they are served with chopped parsley and pepper and salt. The butter should be poured over the potatoes, and supplies the fatty element which potato lacks.

Potatoes à la Maître d'Hôtel.—These are very similar to potato sauté, the difference being that they are not browned at the edges. Small kidney potatoes are best for the purpose. These must be boiled till tender, and the potatoes then cut into slices. These must be warmed up with a spoonful or two of white sauce (*see* WHITE SAUCE), to which is added some chopped parsley and a little lemon-juice. A more common way is to boil the potatoes, slice them up while hot, and then toss them about in a vegetable-dish lightly with a lump of what is called Maître d'Hôtel butter. This is simply a lump of plain cold butter, mixed with chopped parsley, till it looks like a lump of cold parsley and butter. When tossed about squeeze a little lemon-juice over the whole and serve.

Potatoes, New.—New potatoes should be washed and the skin, if necessary, rubbed off with the fingers; they should be thrown into boiling water, slightly salted, and as a rule require from fifteen to five-and-twenty minutes to boil before they are done. During the last few minutes throw in one or two sprigs of fresh mint, drain them off and let them dry, and then place them in a vegetable-dish with the mint and a little piece of butter, in which the potatoes should be boiled to give them a shiny appearance outside.

New potatoes can also be served with a little white sauce to which has been added a little chopped parsley.

Potato Balls.—Mash some boiled potatoes with a little butter, pepper, salt, chopped parsley, chopped onion, or still better, shallot, and add a few savoury herbs. Mix up one or two or more well-beaten eggs, according to the quantity of potato, roll the mixture into balls, flour them, and fry them a nice brown colour, and serve.

Potato Croquettes or Cutlets.—These are very similar to potato balls, only they should be smaller and more delicately flavoured. The potatoes are boiled and mashed, and, if the croquettes are wished to be very good, one or two hard-boiled yolks of eggs should be mixed with them. The mixture is slightly flavoured with shallot, savoury herbs or thyme, chopped parsley, and a little nutmeg. One or two fresh well-beaten-up eggs are now added, the mixture then rolled into small balls no bigger than a walnut. These are then dipped in well-beaten-up egg, and then bread-crumbed. The balls are fried a nice golden-brown colour and served.

Potato cutlets are exactly the same, only instead of shaping the mixture into a little ball, the ball is flattened into the shape of a small oval cutlet. These are then egged, bread-crumbed, and fried, but before being sent to table a small piece of green parsley stalk is stuck in one end to represent the bone of the cutlet. These little cutlets, placed on an ornamental sheet of white paper, at the bottom of the silver dish, look very pretty. A small heap of fried parsley should be placed in the centre of the dish.

Potato Pie.—(*See* SAVOURY DISHES, p. 112.)

Potato Cheesecake.—(*See* CHEESECAKES, p. 169.)

Potato Salads.—(*See* SALADS, p. 101.)

Potato, Border of.—A very pretty dish can be made by making a border of mashed potatoes, hollow in the centre, in which can be placed various kinds of other vegetables, such as haricot beans, stewed peas, &c. The mashed potato should be mixed with one or two well-beaten-up eggs, and the outside of the border can be moulded by hand, to make it look smooth and neat; a piece of flexible tin, flat, will be found very useful, or even a piece of cardboard. If you wish to make the border ornamental, you can proceed exactly as directed under the heading Rice Borders, and if it is wished to make the dish particularly handsome, it can be painted outside, before being placed in the oven, with a yolk of egg beaten up with a tiny drop of hot water. When this is done, the potato border has an appearance similar in colour to the rich pastry generally seen outside a pie, or *vol au vent*. The inside of the potato border after it has been scooped out can be filled with plain boiled macaroni mixed with Parmesan cheese, and ornamented with a little chopped parsley on the top and a few small baked red ripe tomatoes. Again, it can be filled with white haricot beans piled up in the shape of a dome, with some chopped parsley sprinkled over the top. There are, perhaps, few dishes in vegetarian cookery that can be made to look more elegant.

Potato Biscuits (*M. Ude's Recipe*).—Take fifteen fresh eggs, break the yolks into one pan and the whites into another. Beat the yolks with a pound of sugar pounded very fine, scrape the peel of a lemon with a lump of sugar, dry that and pound it fine also; then throw into it the yolks, and work the eggs and sugar till they are of a whitish colour. Next whip the whites well and mix them with the yolks. Now sift half a pound of flour of potatoes through a silk sieve over the eggs and sugar. Have some paper cases ready, which lay on a plafond with some paper underneath. Fill the cases, but not too full; glaze the contents with some rather coarse sugar, and bake the whole in an oven moderately heated.

Potato Bread.—In making bread, a portion of mashed potato is sometimes added to the flour, and this addition improves the bread very much for some tastes; it also keeps it from getting dry quite so soon. At the same time it is not so nutritious as ordinary home-made bread. Boil the required quantity of potatoes in their skins, drain and dry them, then peel and weigh them. Pound them with the rolling-pin until they are quite free from lumps, and mix with them the flour in the proportion of seven pounds of flour to two and a half pounds of potatoes. Add the yeast and knead in the ordinary way, but make up the bread with milk instead of water. When the dough is well risen, bake the bread in a gentle oven. Bake it a little longer than for ordinary bread, and, when it seems done enough, let it stand a little while, with the oven-door open, before taking it out. Unless these precautions are taken, the crust will be hard and brittle, while the inside is still moist and doughy. This recipe is from "Cassell's Dictionary of Cookery."

Potato Cake.—Take a dozen good-sized potatoes and bake them in the oven till done, then peel and put them into a saucepan with a little salt and grated lemon-peel; set them upon the stove and put in a piece of fresh butter and stir the whole; add a little cream and sugar, still continuing to stir them; then let them cool a little and add some orange-flower water, eight yolks of eggs and four only of whites, whisked into froth; heat up the whole together and mix it with the potato purée. Butter a mould and sprinkle it with breadcrumbs; pour in the paste, place the pan upon hot cinders, with fire upon the lid, and let it remain for three-quarters of an hour, or it may be baked in an oven.

Potato Cheese.—Potato cheeses are very highly esteemed in Germany; they can be made of various qualities, but care must be taken that they are not too rich and have not too much heat, or they will burst. Boil the potatoes till they are soft, but the skin must not be broken. The potatoes must be large and of the best quality. When boiled, carefully peel them and beat them to a smooth paste in a mortar with a wooden pestle. To make the commonest cheese, put five pounds of potato paste into a cheese-tub with one pound of milk and rennet; add a sufficient quantity of salt, together with caraways and cumin seed sufficient to impart a good flavour. Knead all these ingredients well together, cover up and allow them to stand three or four days in winter, two to three in summer. At the end of that time knead them again, put the paste into wicker moulds, and leave the cheeses to drain until they are quite dry. When dry and firm, lay them on a board and leave them to acquire hardness gradually in a place of very moderate warmth; should the heat be too great, as we have said, they will burst. When, in spite of all precautions, such accidents occur, the crevices of the burst cheeses are, in Germany, filled with curds and cream mixed, some being also put over the whole surface of the cheese, which is then dried again. As soon as the cheeses are thoroughly dry and hard, place them in barrels with green chickweed between each cheese; let them stand for about three weeks, when they will be fit for use.

Potatoes à la Barigoule.—Peel some potatoes and boil them in a little water with some oil, pepper, salt, onions, and savoury herbs. Boil them slowly, so that they can absorb the liquor; when they are done, brown them in a stew-pan in a little oil, and serve them to be eaten with oil and vinegar, pepper and salt.

Potatoes, Broiled.—Potatoes are served this way sometimes in Italy. They are first boiled in their skins, but not too long. They are then taken out and peeled, cut into thin slices, placed on a gridiron, and grilled till they are crisp. A little oil is poured over them when they are served.

Potatoes à la Lyonnaise.—First boil and then peel and slice some potatoes. Make some rather thin purée of onion. (*See* SAUCE SOUBISE.) Pour this over the potatoes and serve.

Another way is to first brown the slices of potatoes and then serve them with the onion sauce, with the addition of a little vinegar or lemon-juice.

Potatoes à la Provençale.—Put a small piece of butter into a stew-pan, or three tablespoonfuls of oil, three beads of garlic, the peel of a quarter of a lemon, and some parsley, all chopped up very fine; add a little grated nutmeg, pepper and salt. Peel some small potatoes and let them stew till they are tender in this mixture. Large potatoes can be used for the purpose, only they must be cut up into pieces. Add the juice of a lemon before serving.

Haricot Beans.—It is very much to be regretted that haricot beans are not more used in this country. There are hundreds of thousands of families who at the end of a year would be richer in purse and more healthy in body if they would consent to deviate from the beaten track and try haricot beans, not as an accompaniment to a dish of meat, but as an article of diet in themselves. The immense benefit derived in innumerable cases from a diet of beans is one of the strongest and most practical arguments in favour of vegetarianism. Meat-eaters often boast of the plainness of their food, and yet wonder that they suffer in health. It is not an uncommon thing for a man to consult his doctor and to tell him, "I live very simply, nothing but plain roast or boiled."

Medical men are all agreed on one point, and that is that haricot beans rank almost first among vegetables as a nourishing article of diet. In writing on this subject, Sir Henry Thompson observes, "Let me recall, at the close of these few hints about the haricot, the fact that there is no product of the vegetable kingdom so nutritious, holding its own, in this respect, as it well can, even against the beef and mutton of the animal kingdom."

This is a very strong statement, coming as it does from so high an authority, and vegetarians would do well to bear it in mind when discussing the subject of vegetarianism with those who differ from them. Sir Henry proceeds as follows:—
"The haricot ranks just above lentils, which have been so much praised of late, and rightly, the haricot being to most palates more agreeable. By most stomachs, too, haricots are more easily digested than meat is; and, consuming weight for weight, the eater feels lighter and less oppressed, as a rule, after the leguminous dish, while the comparative cost is very greatly in favour of the latter."

To boil haricot beans proceed as follows. We refer, of course, to the dried white haricot beans, the best of which are those known as Soissons. The beans should be soaked in cold water overnight, and in the morning any that may be found floating on the top of the water should be thrown away. Suppose the quantity be a quart; place these in a saucepan with two quarts of cold water, slightly salted. As soon as the water comes to the boil, move it so that the beans will only simmer gently; they must then continue simmering till they are tender. This generally takes about three hours, and if the water is hard, it is advisable to put in a tiny piece of soda. This is the simple way of cooking beans usually recommended in cookery-books when they are served up with a dish of meat, such as a leg of mutton à la Bretonne, where the beans are served in some rich brown gravy containing fat. In vegetarian cookery, of course, we must proceed entirely differently, and there are various ways in which this nourishing dish can be served, as savoury and as appetising, and indeed more so, than if we had assistance from the slaughter-house. We will now proceed to give a few instances.

In the first place, it will greatly assist the flavour of the beans if we boil with them one or two onions and a dessert-spoonful of savoury herbs. Supposing, however, we have them boiled plain. Take a large dry crust of bread and rub the outside well over with one or two heads of garlic. Place this crust of bread with the beans after they have been strained off, and toss them lightly about with the crust without breaking the beans. Remove the crust and moisten the beans while hot with a lump of butter, add a brimming dessertspoonful of chopped blanched parsley; squeeze the juice of a lemon over the whole, and serve. Instead of butter we can add, as they always do in Italy, two or three tablespoonfuls of pure olive oil. Those who have conquered the unreasonable English prejudice against the use of oil will probably find this superior to butter.

If the beans are served in the form of a purée, it is always best to boil a few onions with them and rub the onions through the wire sieve with the beans, taking care that the quantity of onion is not so large that it destroys and overpowers the delicate and delicious flavour of the beans themselves.

Next, we would call attention to the importance of not throwing away the water in which the beans were boiled. This water contains far more nourishment than people are aware of, and throughout the length and breadth of France, where economy is far more understood than in this country, it is invariably saved to assist in making some kind of soup, and as our soup will, of course, be vegetarian, the advantage gained is simply incalculable.

Flageolets.—These are haricot beans in the fresh green state, and are rarely met with in this country, though they form a standing dish abroad. They are exceedingly nice, and can be cooked in a little butter like the French cook green peas. They are often flavoured with garlic, and chopped parsley can be added to them. Those who are fond of this vegetable in the fresh state can obtain them in tins from any high-class grocer, as the leading firms in this country keep them in this form for export.

Peas, Dried.—Dried peas, like dried beans, contain a very great amount of nourishment. Indeed, in this respect, practically, dried beans, dried peas, and lentils may be considered equal. Dried peas are met with in two forms—the split yellow pea and those that are dried whole, green. Split peas are chiefly used in this country to make pea soup, or purée of peas and peas pudding. We have already given recipes for the two former, and will now describe how to make—

Peas Pudding.—Soak a quart of peas in water overnight, throwing away those in the morning that are found floating at the top. Drain them off and tie them up in a pudding-cloth, taking care to leave plenty of room for the peas to swell; put them into cold water, and boil them till they are tender. This will take from two to three hours. When tender, take them out, untie the cloth, and rub them through a colander, or, better still, a wire sieve. Now mix in a couple of ounces of butter with some pepper and salt, flour the cloth well and tie it up again and boil it for another hour, when it can be turned out and served. Peas pudding when eaten alone is improved by mixing in, at the same time as the butter, a dessertspoonful of dried powdered mint, also, should you have the remains of any cold potatoes in the house, it is a very good way of using them up. A few savoury herbs can be used instead of mint.

Peas " Brose."—Dr. Andrew, in writing to the " Cyclopædia of Domestic Medicine," says, " In the West of Scotland, especially in Glasgow, ' peas brose,' as it is called, is made of the fine flour of the white pea, by forming it into a mass merely by the addition of boiling water and a little salt. It is a favourite dish with not only the working classes, but it is even esteemed by many of the gentry. It was introduced into fashion chiefly by the recommendation of Dr. Cleghorn, late Professor of Chemistry in Glasgow University. The peas brose is eaten with milk or butter, and is a sweet, nourishing article of diet peculiarly fitted for persons of a costive habit and for children."

Peas, Dried Whole, Green.—This is perhaps the best form with which we meet peas dried. When the best quality is selected, and care taken in their preparation, they are quite equal to fresh green peas when they are old. Indeed, many persons prefer them.

Soak the peas overnight, throwing away those that float at the top; put them into cold water, and when they boil let the peas simmer gently till they are tender. The time varies very much with the quality and the size of the peas, old ones requiring nearly three hours, others considerably less. When the peas are tender, throw in some sprigs, if possible, of fresh mint, and after a minute strain them off; add pepper, salt, and about two ounces of butter to a quart of peas—though this is not absolutely necessary—and nearly a dessertspoonful of white powdered sugar.

If you wish to have the peas as bright a green as freshly gathered ones, after you strain them off you can mix them in a basin, before you add the butter, with a little piece of green vegetable colouring (sold in bottles by all grocers). The peas should then be put back in the saucepan for a few minutes to be made hot through, and then finished as directed before.

Peas, Dried, Green, with Cream.—Boil the peas as before directed till they are quite tender, then strain them off and put them in a stew-pan with one ounce of butter to every quart of peas and toss them lightly about with a little pepper, salt, and grated nutmeg. Add to each quart of peas a quarter of a pint of cream and a dessertspoonful of powdered sugar; surround the dish with fried or toasted bread.

Lentils.—Lentils are, comparatively speaking, a novel form of food in this country, though they have been used abroad for many years, and a recipe for cooking them will be found in a well-known work, published in Paris in 1846, entitled "*La Cuisinière de la Campagne et de la Ville; ou, Nouvelle Cuisine Économique*," one of the most popular French cookery-books ever published, and which in that year had reached a circulation of 80,000 copies.

Recipes for boiled lentils and lentil soup are given in "Cassell's Dictionary of Cookery," published in 1875; but it is stated in the introductory remarks that lentils are little used in England except as food for pigeons, and adds, "They are seldom offered for sale." Since that date lentils have become an exceedingly popular form of food in many households, and vegetarians generally regard them as one of the most nourishing forms of food served at the table. There are two kinds of lentils, the German and Egyptian. The Egyptian are red and much smaller than the German, which are green. The former kind are generally used on the Continent, in Italy and the South of France, while, as the name implies, the green lentils are more commonly used in Eastern Europe. Either kind, however, can be used for making soup and purée, recipes of which have already been given, as well as for the recipes in the present chapter.

Lentils, Boiled.—The lentils should be placed in soak overnight, and those that float should be thrown away. Suppose we have half a pint of lentils, they should be boiled in about a pint and a half of water. Boil them till they are tender, which will take about half an hour, then drain them off and put them back in the saucepan for a few minutes with a little piece of butter, squeeze over them the juice of half a lemon, and serve hot. Some people make a little thickened sauce with yolks of eggs and a little butter and flour mixed with the water in which they are boiled.

Lentils, Curried.—Lentils are very nice curried. Boil the lentils as directed above till they are tender. When they are placed in a vegetable-dish make a deep well in the centre and pour some thick curry sauce into it. (*See* CURRY SAUCE.)

Lentils à la Provençale.—Soak the lentils overnight and put them into a stew-pan with five or six spoonfuls of oil, a little butter, some slices of onion, some chopped parsley, and a teaspoonful of mixed savoury herbs. Stew them in this till the lentils are tender, and then thicken the sauce with yolks of eggs, add a squeeze of lemon-juice, and serve.

N.B.—Haricot beans can be cooked in a similar manner.

CHAPTER VIII.

VEGETABLES, FRESH.

Artichokes, French, Plain Boiled.—Put the artichokes to soak in some well salted water, upside down, as otherwise it is impossible to get rid of the insects that are sometimes hidden in the leaves. Trim off the ends of the leaves and the stalk, and all the hard leaves round the bottom should be pulled off. Put the artichokes into a saucepan of boiling water sufficiently deep to nearly cover them. The tips of the leaves are best left out; add a little salt, pepper, and a spoonful of savoury herbs to the water in which they are boiled. French cooks generally add a piece of butter. Boil them till they are tender. The time depends upon the size, but you can always tell when they are done by pulling out a single leaf. If it comes out easily the artichokes are done. Drain them off, and remember in draining them to turn them upside down. Some kind of sauce is generally served with artichokes separately in a boat, such as butter sauce, sauce Allemande, or Dutch sauce.

Artichokes, Broiled.—Parboil the artichokes and take out the part known as the choke. In the hollow place a little chopped parsley and light-coloured bread-raspings soaked in olive oil. Place the bottoms of the artichokes on a gridiron with narrow bars over a clear fire, and serve them as soon as they are thoroughly hot through.

Artichokes, Fried.—The bottoms of artichokes after being boiled can be dipped in batter and fried.

Artichokes à la Provençale.—Parboil the artichokes and remove the choke, and put them in the oven in a tin with a little oil, pepper and salt, and three or four heads of garlic, whole. Let them bake till they are tender, turning them over in the oil occasionally; then take out the garlic and serve them with the oil poured over them, and add the juice of a lemon.

Artichokes, Jerusalem, Boiled, Plain.—The artichokes

must be first washed and peeled, and should be treated like potatoes in this respect. They should be thrown into cold water immediately, and it is best to add a little vinegar to the water. If the artichokes are young, throw them into boiling water, and they will become tender in about a quarter of an hour or twenty minutes. It is very important not to over-boil them, as they turn a bad colour. If any doubt exists as to the age of the artichokes, they had better be tested with a fork. Immediately they are tender they should be drained and served.

Old artichokes must be treated like old potatoes, *i.e.*, put originally into cold water, and when they come to the boiling point allowed to simmer till tender; but these are best mashed. When the artichokes have been drained, they can, of course, be served quite plain, but they are best sent to table with some kind of sauce poured over them, such as Allemande sauce, Dutch sauce, white sauce, or plain butter sauce. They are greatly improved in appearance, after a spoonful of sauce has been poured over each artichoke, if a little blanched chopped parsley is sprinkled over them, and a few red specks made by colouring a pinch of bread-crumbs by shaking them with a few drops of cochineal.

Another very nice way of sending artichokes to table is to place all the artichokes together in a vegetable-dish, and, after pouring a little white sauce over each artichoke, to place a fresh-boiled bright green Brussels sprout between each. The white and green contrast very prettily.

Jerusalem Artichokes, Fried.—Peel and slice the artichokes very thin; throw these slices into smoking hot oil in which a frying-basket has been placed. As soon as the artichokes are of bright golden-brown colour, lift out the frying-basket, shake it while you pepper and salt the artichokes, and serve very hot. They can be eaten with thin brown bread-and-butter and lemon-juice, and form a sort of vegetarian whitebait.

Artichokes, Mashed.—These are best made from old artichokes. They must be rubbed through a wire sieve, and the strings left behind. It is best to mash them up with a little butter, and a spoonful or two of cream is a very great improvement.

Asparagus, Boiled.—Cut the asparagus all the same length by bringing the green points together, and then trimming the stalks level with a sharp knife. Throw the asparagus into boiling salted water. Time, from fifteen to twenty-five minutes, according to thickness. Serve on dry toast, and send butter sauce to table separate in a tureen.

Beans, Broad, Plain Boiled.—Broad beans, if eaten whole, should be quite young. They should be thrown into boiling water, salted. They require about twenty minutes to boil before they are tender. Serve with parsley and butter sauce.

Broad Beans, Mashed.—When broad beans get old, the only way to serve them is to have them mashed. Boil them, and remove the skins, then mash them up with a little butter, pepper, and salt, and rub them through a wire sieve, make them hot, and serve. You can if you like boil a few green onions and a pinch of savoury herbs with the beans, and rub these through the wire sieve as well. This dish is very cheap and very nourishing. Very young beans, like very young peas, are more nice than economical.

Beans à la Poulette.—Boil some young beans till they are tender, and put them into a saucepan with a little butter, sugar, pepper, and salt, and sufficient flour to prevent the butter cooking oily; stew them in this a short time, *i.e.*, till they appear to begin to boil, as the water from the beans will mix with the butter and flour and look like thin butter sauce; thicken this with one or two yolks of eggs, and serve.

Beans à la Bourgeoise.—Place the beans in a saucepan, with a piece of butter, a small quantity of shallot chopped fine, and a teaspoonful of savoury herbs; toss them about in this a little time, and then add a little water, sufficient to moisten them so that they can stew; add a little sugar, and when tender thicken the water with some beaten-up egg.

Beans, French, Plain Boiled.—French beans are only good when fresh gathered, and the younger they are the better. When small they can be boiled whole, in which case they only require the tips cut off and the string that runs down the side removed. When they are more fully grown they will require, in addition to being trimmed in this manner, to be cut into thin strips, and when very old it will be found best to cut them slanting. They must be thrown into boiling salted water, and boiled till they are tender. The time for boiling varies with the age; very young ones will not take more than a quarter of an hour, and if old ones are not tender in half an hour they had better be made into a purée. As soon as the beans are tender, drain them off, and serve them very hot; the chief point to bear in mind, if we wish to have our beans nice, is, they must be eaten directly they are drained from the water in which they are boiled. They are spoilt by what is called being kept hot, and possess a marvellous facility of getting cold in a very short space of time.

In vegetarian cookery, when beans are eaten without being an accompaniment to meat, some form of fat is desirable. When the beans are drained we can add either butter or oil. When a lump of *Maître d'Hôtel* butter is added they form what the French call *haricots vert à la Maître d'Hôtel*. In this case, a slight suspicion of garlic may be added by rubbing the stew-pan in which the French beans are tossed together with the *Maître d'Hôtel* butter. When oil is added, a little chopped parsley will be found an improvement, as well as pepper, salt, and a suspicion of nutmeg.

French beans are very nice flavoured with oil and garlic, and served in a border of macaroni.

French Bean Pudding.—When French beans are very old they are sometimes made into a pudding as follows:—They must be trimmed. cut up, boiled, with or without the addition of a few savoury herbs. They must be then mashed in a basin, tied up in a well-buttered and then floured cloth, and boiled for some time longer. The pudding can then be turned out. A still better way of making a French bean pudding is to rub the beans through the wire sieve, leaving the strings behind, flavouring the pudding with a few savoury herbs, a little sugar, pepper, and salt, and, if liked, a suspicion of garlic; add one or two well-beaten-up eggs, and put the mixture in a round pudding-basin, and bake it till it sets. This can be turned out on the centre of a dish, and a few young French beans placed round the base to ornament it, in conjunction with some pieces of fried bread cut into pretty shapes.

VEGETABLES, FRESH. 141

Brocoli.—Trim the outer leaves off a brocoli, and cut off the stalk even, so that it will stand upright. Soak the brocoli in salt and water for some time, in order to get rid of any insects. Throw the brocoli into boiling water that has been salted, and boil till it is tender, the probable time for young brocoli being about a quarter of an hour. It should be served on a dish with the flower part uppermost; and butter sauce, sauce Allemande, or Dutch sauce can be served separately, or poured over the surface.

When several heads of brocoli are served at once, it is important to cut the stalks flat, as directed, before boiling. After they have been thoroughly drained *upside down*, they should be placed on the dish, flower part uppermost, and placed together as much as possible to look like one large brocoli. If sauce is poured over them, the sauce should be sufficiently thick to be spread, and every part of the flower should be covered. Half a teaspoonful of chopped blanched parsley may be sprinkled over the top, and improves the appearance of the dish.

N.B.—We would particularly call attention to the importance of draining brocoli and cauliflower very thoroughly, especially when any sauce is served with the brocoli. When the dish is cut into, nothing looks more disagreeable than to see the white sauce running off the brocoli into green water at the bottom of the dish.

Brocoli Greens.—The outside leaves of brocoli should not be thrown away, but eaten. Too often they are trimmed off at the greengrocer's or at the market, and, we presume, utilised for the purpose of feeding cattle. They can be boiled exactly like white cabbages, and are equal to them, if not superior, in flavour. To boil them, *see* CABBAGE, WHITE, LARGE.

Brussels Sprouts.—These must be first washed in cold water and all the little pieces of decayed leaves trimmed away. Throw them into boiling salted water; the water must be kept boiling the whole time, without a lid on the saucepan, and if the quantity of water be sufficiently large not to be taken off the boil by the sprouts being thrown in they will be sent to table of a far brighter green colour than otherwise. In order to ensure this, throw in the sprouts a few at a time, picking out the big ones to throw in first. Sprouts, as soon as they are tender—probable time a quarter of an hour—should be drained and served *quickly*. When served as a dish by themselves, after being drained off, they can be placed in a stew-pan with a little butter, pepper, salt, nutmeg, and lemon-juice. They can then be served with toasted or fried bread.

Cabbage, Plain Boiled.—Ordinary young cabbages should be first trimmed by having the outside leaves removed, the stalks cut off, and then should be cut in halves and allowed to soak some time in salt and water. They should be thrown into plenty of boiling water; the water should be kept boiling and uncovered. As soon as they are tender they should be strained off and served *immediately*. Young summer cabbages will not take longer than a quarter of an hour, or even less; old cabbages take nearly double that time. It is impossible to lay down any exact rule with regard to time. Savoys generally take about half an hour. The large white cabbages met with in the West of England take longer and require a different treatment.

When cabbage is served as a dish by itself it will be found a great improvement to add either butter or oil to moisten the cabbage after it is thoroughly drained off. In order to ensure the butter not oiling, but adhering to the cabbage, it is best after the butter is added, and while you mix it with the cabbage, to shake the flour-dredger two or three times over the vegetable. In Germany, many add vinegar and sugar to the cabbage.

Cabbage, Large White.—In the West of England cabbages grow to an immense size, owing, probably, to the moist heat, and have been exhibited in agricultural shows over twenty pounds in weight and as big as an eighteen gallon cask. These cabbages are best boiled as follows :—After being cut up and thoroughly washed, it will be found that the greater part of the cabbage resembles what in ordinary cabbage would be called stalk, and, of course, the leaves vary very considerably in thickness from the hard stalk end up to the leaf. Have plenty of boiling water ready salted, now cut off the stalk part where it is thickest and throw this in first. Wait till the water comes to the boil again and let it boil for a few minutes. Then throw in the next thickest part and again wait till the water re-boils, and so on, reserving the thin leafy part to be thrown in last of all. By this means, and this only, do we get the cabbage boiled uniformly. Had we thrown in all at once one of two things would be inevitable—either the stalk would be too hard to be eaten or the leafy part over-boiled. A large white cabbage takes about an hour to boil tender, and a piece of soda should be added to the water. When the cabbage is well drained, it can be served either plain or moistened, and made to look oily by the addition of a piece of butter. As the cabbage is very white, the dish is very much improved by the addition of a little chopped parsley sprinkled over the top, not for the sake of flavour but appearance.

Cabbage and Cream.—Ordinary cabbages are sometimes served stewed with a little cream. They should be first parboiled, then the moisture squeezed from them, and then they must be put in a stew-pan with a little butter, pepper, salt and nutmeg, and a spoonful of flour should be shaken over the cabbage in order to prevent the butter being too oily. When the cabbage is stewed till it is perfectly tender, add a few spoonfuls of cream, stir up, and make the whole thoroughly hot, and serve with fried or toasted bread.

Cabbage, Red.—Red cabbages are chiefly used for pickling. They are sometimes served fresh. They should be cut across so that the cabbage shreds, boiled till they are tender, the moisture thoroughly extracted, and then put into a stew-pan with a little butter, pepper, and salt, and a few shakes of flour from the flour-dredger. After stirring for ten minutes or a quarter of an hour, squeeze the juice of a lemon over them and serve.

Carrots, Boiled.—When carrots are boiled and served as a course by themselves, they ought to be young. This dish is constantly met with abroad in early summer, but is rarely seen in England, except at the tables of vegetarians. The carrots should be trimmed, thoroughly washed, and, if necessary, slightly scraped, and the point at the end, which looks like a piece of string, should be cut off. They should be thrown into fast boiling water (salted) in order to preserve their colour. When tender they can be served with some kind of good white sauce, or sauce Allemande or Dutch sauce. Perhaps this latter sauce is best of all, as it looks like rich custard. Part of the red carrot should show uncovered by any sauce. They are best placed in a circle and the thick sauce poured in the centre; a very little chopped blanched parsley can be sprinkled on the top of the sauce. In making Dutch sauce for carrots use lemon-juice instead of tarragon vinegar.

Carrots, Fried.—Fried carrots can be made from full-grown carrots. They must be first parboiled and then cut in slices; they must then be dipped in well-beaten-up egg, and then covered with fine dry bread-crumbs and fried a nice brown in smoking hot oil in a frying-basket. The slices of carrot should be peppered and salted before being dipped in the egg.

Carrots, Mashed.—When carrots are very old they are best mashed. Boil them for some time, then cut them up and rub them through a wire sieve. They can be pressed in a basin and made hot by being steamed. A little butter, pepper and salt should be added to the mixture. A very pretty dish can be made by means of mixing mashed carrots with mashed turnips. They can be shaped in a basin, and with a little ingenuity can be put into red and white stripes. The effect is something like the top of a striped tent.

Cauliflower, Plain Boiled.—Cauliflowers can be treated in exactly the same manner as brocoli, and there are very few who can tell the difference. (*See* BROCOLI.)

Cauliflower au gratin.—This is a very nice method of serving cauliflower as a course by itself. The cauliflower or cauliflowers should first be boiled till thoroughly tender, very carefully drained, and then placed upright in a vegetable-dish with the flower part uppermost. The whole of the flower part should then be *masked* (*i.e.*, covered over) with some thick white sauce. Allemande sauce or Dutch sauce will do. This is then sprinkled over with grated Parmesan cheese and the dish put in the oven for the top to brown. As soon as it *begins* to brown take it out of the oven and finish it off neatly with a salamander (a red-hot shovel will do), the same way you finish cheese-cakes made from curds.

Cauliflower and Tomato Sauce.—Boil and place the cauliflower or flowers upright in a dish as in the above recipe. Now mask all the flower part very neatly, commencing round the edges first, with some tomato conserve previously made warm, and serve immediately. This is a very pretty-looking dish.

Celery, Stewed.—The secret of having good stewed celery is only to cook the white part. Throw the celery into boiling water, with only sufficient water just to cover it. When the celery is tender use some of the water in which it is stewed to make a sauce to serve with it, or better still, stew the celery in milk. The sauce looks best when it is thickened with the yolks of eggs. A very nice sauce indeed can be made by first thickening the milk or water in which the celery is stewed with a little white roux, and then adding a quarter of a pint of cream boiled separately. Stewed celery should be served on toast, like asparagus; a little chopped blanched parsley can be sprinkled over the white sauce by way of ornament, and fried bread should be placed round the edge of the dish.

Stewed celery can also be served with sauce Allemande or Dutch sauce.

Endive.—Endive is generally used as a salad, but is very nice served as a vegetable, stewed. White-heart endives should be chosen, and several heads will be required for a dish, as they shrink very much in cooking. Wash and clean the endives very carefully in salt and water first, as they often contain insects. Boil them in slightly salted water till they are tender, then drain them off, and thoroughly extract the moisture; put them in a stew-pan with a little butter, pepper, salt, and nutmeg, let them stew for some little time; add the juice of a lemon, and serve. It will make the dish much prettier if you reserve one head of endive boiled whole. Place the stewed endive on a dish, and sprinkle some chopped blanched parsley over it, then place the single head of endive upright in the centre, and place some fried bread round the edge.

Leeks, Stewed.—Leeks must be trimmed down to where the green part meets the white on the one side, and the root, where the strings are, cut off on the other. They should be thrown into boiling water, boiled till they are tender, and then

F

thoroughly drained. The water in which leeks have been boiled is somewhat rank and bitter, and, as the leeks are like tubes, in order to drain them perfectly you must turn them upside down. They can be served on toast, and covered with some kind of white sauce, either ordinary white sauce, sauce Allemande, or Dutch sauce.

Leeks, Welsh Porridge.—The leeks are stewed and cut in slices, and served in some of the liquor in which they are boiled, with toast cut in strips, something like onion porridge. Boil the leeks for five minutes, drain them off, and throw away the first water, and then stew them gently in some fresh water. In years back, in Wales, French plums were stewed with and added to the porridge.

Lettuces, Stewed.—As lettuces shrink very much when boiled, allowance must be made, and several heads used. This is also a very good way of utilising the large old-fashioned English lettuce resembling in shape a gingham umbrella. They should be first boiled till tender. The time depends entirely upon the size. Drain them off, and thoroughly extract the moisture; put them into a stew-pan, with a little butter, pepper, salt, and nutmeg. Let them stew some little time, and add a little vinegar, or, still better, lemon-juice.

Lettuces Stewed with Peas.—A border of stewed lettuces can be made as above, and the centre filled up with some fresh-boiled young green peas.

Onions, Plain Boiled.—When onions are served as a dish by themselves, Spanish onions are far best for the purpose. Ordinary onions, as a rule, are too strong to be eaten, except as an accompaniment to some other kind of food. When onions are plain boiled, they are best served on dry toast without any sauce at all. Butter can be added when eaten on the plate if liked. Large Spanish onions will require about three hours to boil tender.

Onions, Baked.—Spanish onions can be baked in the oven. They are best placed in saucers, with a very little butter to prevent them sticking, with which they can also be basted occasionally. Probable time about three hours. They should be of a nice brown colour at the finish.

Onions, Stewed.—Place a large Spanish onion in a saucer at the bottom of the saucepan, and put sufficient water in the saucepan to reach the edge of the saucer; keep the lid of the saucepan on tight, and let it steam till tender. A large onion would take about three hours. The water from the onion will prevent the necessity of adding fresh water from time to time.

Parsnips.—Like young carrots, young parsnips are often met with abroad as a course by themselves. They should be trimmed and boiled whole, and served with white sauce, Allemande sauce, or Dutch sauce; a little chopped blanched parsley should be sprinkled over the sauce, and fried bread served round the edge of the dish.

Parsnips, Fried.—Boil some full-grown parsnips till they are tender, cut them into slices, pepper and salt them, dip them into beaten-up egg, and cover them with bread-crumbs, and fry these slices in some smoking hot oil till they are a nice brown colour.

Parsnips, Mashed.—When parsnips are very old they are best mashed. Boil them for an hour or more, then cut them up and rub them through a wire sieve. The stringy part will have to be left behind. Mix the pulp with a little butter, pepper, and salt; make this hot, and serve. A little cream is a great improvement.

Parsnip Cake.—Boil two or three parsnips until they are tender enough to mash, then press them through a colander with the back of a wooden spoon, and carefully remove any fibrous, stringy pieces there may be. Mix a teacupful of the mashed parsnip with a quart of hot milk, add a teaspoonful of salt, four ounces of fresh butter, half a pint of yeast, and enough flour to make a stiff batter. Put the bowl which contains the mixture in a warm place, cover it with a cloth, and leave it to rise. When it has risen to twice its original size, knead some more flour into it, and let it rise again; make it into small round cakes a quarter of an inch thick, and place these on buttered tins. Let them stand before the fire a few minutes, and bake them in a hot oven. They do not taste of the parsnip. Time, some hours to rise; about twenty minutes to bake.

Peas, Green.—By far the best and nicest way of cooking green peas when served as a course by themselves is to stew them gently in a little butter without any water at all, like they do in France. The peas are first shelled, and then placed in a stew-pan with a little butter, sufficient to moisten them. As soon as they are tender, which will vary with the size and age of the peas, they can be served just as they are. The flavour of peas cooked this way is so delicious that they are nicest eaten with plain bread. When old peas are cooked this way it is customary to add a little white powdered sugar.

Peas, Green, Plain Boiled.—Shell the peas, and throw them into boiling water slightly salted. Keep the lid off the saucepan and throw in a few sprigs of fresh green mint five minutes before you drain them off. Young peas will take about ten to twenty minutes, and full-grown peas rather longer. Serve the peas directly they are drained, as they are spoilt by being kept hot.

Peas, Stewed.—When peas late in the season get old and tough, they can be stewed. Boil them for rather more than half an hour, throwing them first of all into boiling water; drain them off, and put them into a stew-pan with a little butter, pepper, and salt. Young onions and lettuces cut up can be stewed with them, but young green peas are far too nice ever to be spoilt by being cooked in this way.

Scotch Kale.—Scotch kale, or curly greens, as it is sometimes called in some parts of the country, is cooked like ordinary greens. It should be washed very carefully, and thrown into fast-boiling salted water. The saucepan should remain uncovered, as we wish to preserve the dark green colour. Young Scotch kale will take about twenty minutes to boil before it is tender. When boiled, if served as a course by itself, it should be strained off very thoroughly and warmed in a stew-pan with a little butter, pepper, and salt.

Sea Kale.—Sea kale possesses a very delicate flavour, and in cooking it the endeavour should be to preserve this flavour. Throw the sea kale when washed into boiling water; in about twenty minutes, if it is young, it will be tender. Serve it on plain dry toast, and keep all the heads one way. Butter sauce, white sauce, Dutch sauce, or sauce Allemande can be served with sea kale, but should be sent to table separate in a boat, as the majority of good judges prefer the sea kale quite plain.

Spinach.—The chief difficulty to contend with in cooking spinach is the preliminary cleansing. The best method of washing spinach is to take two buckets of water. Wash it in one; the spinach will float on the top whilst the dirt settles at the bottom. Lift the spinach from one pail, after you have allowed it to settle for a few minutes, into the other pail. One or two rinsings will be sufficient. Spinach should be picked if the stalks are large, and thrown into boiling water slightly salted. Boil the spinach till it is tender, which will take about a quarter of an hour, then drain it off and cut it very small in a basin with a knife and fork, place it back in a saucepan with a little piece of butter to make it thoroughly hot, put it in a vegetable dish and serve.

Hard-boiled eggs cut in halves, or poached eggs, are usually served with spinach. A little cream, nutmeg, and lemon-juice can be added. Many cooks rub the spinach through a wire sieve.

Vegetable Marrow.—Vegetable marrows must be first peeled, cut open, the pips removed, and then thrown into boiling water; small ones should be cut into quarters and large ones into pieces about as big as the palm of the hand. They take from fifteen to twenty minutes to boil before they are tender. They should be served directly they are cooked and placed on dry toast. Butter sauce or white sauce can be served with them, but is best sent to table separate in a boat, as many persons prefer them plain.

Vegetable Marrows, Stuffed.—Young vegetable marrows are very nice stuffed. They should be first peeled very slightly and then cut, long-ways, into three zigzag slices; the pips should be removed and the interior filled with either mushroom forcemeat (*see* MUSHROOM FORCEMEAT) or sage-and-onion stuffing made with rather an extra quantity of bread-crumbs. The vegetable marrow should be tied up with two separate loops of tape about a quarter of the way from each end, and these two rings of tape tied together with two or three separate pieces of tape to prevent them slipping off at the ends. The forcemeat or stuffing should be made hot before it is placed in the marrow. The vegetable marrow should now be thrown into boiling water and boiled till it is tender, about twenty minutes to half an hour. Take off the tape carefully, and be careful to place the marrow so that one half rests on the other half, or else it will slip.

N.B.—If you place the stuffing inside cold, the vegetable marrow will break before the inside gets hot through.

Turnips, Boiled.—When turnips are young they are best boiled whole. Peel them first very thinly, and throw them into cold water till they are ready for the saucepan. Throw them into boiling water slightly salted. They will probably take about twenty minutes to boil. They can be served quite plain or with any kind of white sauce, butter sauce, sauce Allemande, or Dutch sauce. In vegetarian cookery they are perhaps best served with some other kind of vegetable.

Turnips, Mashed.—Old turnips are best mashed, as they are stringy. Boil them till they get fairly tender; they will take from half an hour to two hours, according to age; then rub them through a wire sieve and warm up the pulp with a little milk, or still better, cream and a little butter; add pepper and salt.

N.B.—If the pulp be very moist let it stand and get rid of the moisture gradually in a frying-pan over a very slack fire.

Turnips, Ornamental.—A very pretty way of serving young turnips in vegetarian cookery is to cut them in halves and scoop out the centre so as to form cups; the part scooped out can be mixed with some carrot cut up into small pieces, and some green peas, and placed in the middle of a dish in a heap; the half-turnips forming cups can be placed round the base of the dish and each cup filled alternately with the red part of the carrot, chopped small and piled up, and a spoonful of green peas. This makes a very pretty dish of mixed vegetables.

Turnip-tops.—Turnip-tops, when fresh cut, make very nice and wholesome greens. They should be thrown into boiling water and boiled for about twenty minutes, when they will be tender. They should then be cut up with a knife and fork very finely and served like spinach. If rubbed through a wire sieve and a little spinach extract mixed with them to give them the proper colour, and served with hard-boiled eggs, there are very few persons who can distinguish the dish from eggs and spinach.

Vegetable Curry.—A border made of all kinds of mixed vegetables is very nice sent to table with some good thick curry sauce poured in the centre.

Nettles, To Boil.—The best time to gather nettles for eating purposes is in the early spring. They are freely eaten in many parts of the country, as they are considered excellent for purifying the blood. The young light-green leaves only should be taken. They must be washed carefully and boiled in two waters, a little salt and a very small piece of soda being put in the last water. When tender, turn them into a colander, press the water from them, put them into a hot vegetable-dish, score them across three or four times, and serve. Send melted butter to table in a tureen. Time, about a quarter of an hour to boil.

Salsify.—Scrape the salsify and throw it into cold water with a little vinegar. Then throw it into boiling water, boil till tender, and serve on toast with white sauce. Time to boil, about one hour.

CHAPTER IX.

PRESERVED VEGETABLES AND FRUITS.

VEGETABLES and fruits are preserved in two ways. We can have them preserved both in bottles and tins, but the principle is exactly the same in both cases, the method of preservation being simply that of excluding the air. We will not enter into the subject of how to preserve fruit and vegetables, but will confine ourselves to discussing as briefly as possible the best method of using them when they are preserved.

Unfortunately there exists a very unreasonable prejudice on the part of many persons against all kinds of provisions that are preserved in tins. This prejudice is kept alive by stories that occasionally get into print about families being poisoned by using tinned goods. We hear stories also of poisoning resulting from using copper vessels. Housekeepers should endeavour to grasp the idea that the evil is the result of their own ignorance, and that no danger would accrue were they possessed of a little more elementary knowledge of chemistry. If a penny be dipped in vinegar and exposed to the air, and is then licked by a child, a certain amount of ill effect would undoubtedly ensue, but it does not follow that we should give up the use of copper money. So, too, if we use tinned goods, and owing to our own carelessness or ignorance find occasionally that evil results ensue, we should not give up the use of the goods in question, but endeavour to find out the cause why these evil results follow only occasionally.

All good cooks know, or ought to know, that if they leave the soup all night in a saucepan the soup is spoilt. Again, all housekeepers know that although they have a metal tank, they are bound to have a wooden lid on top, there being a law to this effect. The point they forget in using tinned goods is this, so long as the air is excluded from the interior of the

PRESERVED VEGETABLES AND FRUITS. 153

tin no chemical action goes on whatever. When, therefore, they open the tin, if they turn out the contents at once no harm can ensue. Unfortunately, there are many thousands who will open a tin, take out what they want, and *leave the remainder in the tin.* Of course, they have only themselves to blame should evil result.

Preserved vegetables are so useful that they are inseparable from civilised cookery; for instance, what would a French cook do were he dependent for his mushrooms upon those fresh grown in the fields? The standard dish at vegetarian restaurants is mushroom pie, and, thanks to tinned mushrooms, we can obtain this dish all the year round. In most restaurants peas are on the bill of fare throughout the year. Were we dependent upon fresh grown ones, this popular dish would be confined almost to a few weeks.

In the case of preserved goods, tinned fruits are even more valuable than tinned vegetables. Ripe apricots and peaches picked fresh from the tree are expensive luxuries that in this country can only be indulged in by the rich, whereas, thanks to the art of preserving, we are enabled to enjoy them all the year round. We will run briefly through a few of the chief vegetables and fruits, and give a few hints how to best use them. First of all—

Asparagus, Tinned.—Place the tin in the saucepan with sufficient cold water to cover it. Bring the water to a boil and let it boil for five minutes; take out the tin and cut it open round the edge, as near to the edge as possible, otherwise you will be apt to break the asparagus in turning it out. Drain off the liquor and serve the asparagus on freshly made hot toast. There is much less waste as a rule in tinned asparagus than in that freshly cut. As a rule, you can eat nearly the whole of it.

Peas, Tinned.—Put the tin before it is opened into cold water, bring the water to a boil, and let it boil five minutes, or longer if the tin is a large one. Cut open the tin at the top, pour out the liquor, and serve the peas with a few sprigs of fresh mint, if it can be obtained, that have been boiled for two or three minutes. Supposing the tin to contain a pint of peas, add while the peas are thoroughly hot a brimming saltspoonful of finely powdered sugar, and half a saltspoonful of salt. If the peas are to be eaten by themselves, as is generally the case with vegetarians, add a good-sized piece of butter.

French Beans, Tinned.—These can be treated in exactly a similar manner to green peas, only, instead of adding mint, add a little chopped blanched parsley; the same quantity of sugar and salt should be added as in the case of peas. After the butter has melted, it is a great improvement, when the beans are eaten as a course by themselves, with bread, if the juice of half a lemon is added.

Flageolets, Tinned.—For this delicious vegetable, in England, we are dependent upon tinned goods, as we cannot recall an instance in which they can be bought freshly gathered. Warm up the beans in the tin by placing the tin in cold water, bringing the water to a boil, and letting it boil for five minutes. Drain off the liquor, add a saltspoonful of sugar, half a one of salt, and a lump of butter. Instead of butter, you can add to each pint two tablespoonfuls of pure olive oil. Many persons consider it a great improvement to rub the vegetable-dish with a bead of garlic. In this case the beans should be tossed about in the dish for a minute or two.

Brussels Sprouts, Tinned.—The tin should be made hot before it is opened, the liquor drained off, and the sprouts placed in a dish, with a little butter or oil, powdered sugar, salt, pepper, and a slight flavouring of nutmeg. In France, in some parts, a little cream is poured over them.

Spinach, Tinned.—Spinach is sold in tins fairly cheap, and, quoting from the list of a large retail establishment where prices correspond with those of the Civil Service Stores, a tin of spinach can be obtained for fivepence-halfpenny. The spinach should be made very hot in the tin, turned out on to a dish, and hard-boiled eggs, hot, cut in halves, added. Some people add also a little vinegar, but, unless persons' tastes are known beforehand, that is best added on the plate.

Carrots, Tinned.—Young carrots can be obtained in tins, and, as only young carrots are nice when served as a course by themselves, these will be found a valuable addition to the vegetarian store-cupboard. Make the carrots hot in the tin, and let the water boil for quite ten minutes after it comes to the boiling point. Drain off the liquor, and serve them with some kind of white sauce exactly as if they were freshly boiled young carrots.

Turnips, Tinned.—Proceed exactly the same as in the case of carrots.

Fond d'Artichoke.—These consist of the bottom part only of French artichokes. They should be made hot in the tin, and served up with some good butter sauce, and cut lemon separate, as many prefer the artichokes plain.

Macedoines.—This, as the word implies, is a mixture of various vegetables, the chief of which are generally chopped-up carrot and turnip with young green peas. A very nice dish which can be served at a very short notice, if you have curry sauce in bottles, is a dish of vegetable curry. The macedoines should be made hot in the tin, the liquor drained off, and the curry sauce, made hot, should be poured into a well made in the centre of the macedoines in the dish. Macedoines are also very useful, as they can be served as a vegetable salad at a moment's notice, as the vegetables are sufficiently cooked without being made hot.

Tinned Fruits.—Tinned fruits are ready for eating directly the tin is opened. All we have to bear in mind is to turn them all out of the tin on to a dish immediately. Do not leave any in the tin to be used at another time. Most tinned fruits can be served just as they are, in a glass dish, but a great improvement can be made in their appearance at a very small cost and with a very little extra trouble if we always have in the house a little preserved angelica and a few dried cherries. As these cost about a shilling or one and fourpence per pound, and even a quarter of a pound is sufficient to ornament two or three dozen dishes, the extra expense is almost nil.

Apricots, Tinned.—Pile the apricots up, with the convex side uppermost, in a glass dish, reserving one cup apricot to go on the top, with the concave side uppermost. Take a few preserved cherries, and cut them in halves, and stick half a cherry in all the little holes or spaces where the apricots meet. Cut four little green leaves out of the angelica about the size of the thumb-nail, only a little longer; the size of a filbert would perhaps describe the size better. Put a whole cherry in the apricot cup at the top, and four green leaves of angelica round it. Take the white kernel of the apricot—one or two will always be found in every tin—and cut four white slices out of the middle, place these round the red cherry, touching the cherry, and resting between the four green leaves of angelica; the top of this dish has now the appearance of a very pretty flower.

Peaches, Tinned.—These can be treated in exactly a similar way to the apricots.

Peaches and Apricots, with Cream.—Place the fruit in a glass dish, with the concave side uppermost; pour the syrup round the fruit, and with a teaspoon remove any syrup that may have settled in the little cups, for such the half-peaches or apricots may be called. Get a small jar of Devonshire clotted cream; take about half a teaspoonful of cream, and place it in the middle of each cup, and place a single preserved cherry on the top of the cream. This dish can be made still prettier by chopping up a little green angelica, like parsley, and sprinkling a few of these little green specks on the white cream.

Pine-apple, Tinned.—Pine-apples are preserved in tins whole, and are very superior in flavour to those which are sold cheap on barrows, which are more rotten than ripe. They require very little ornamenting, but the top is greatly improved by placing a red cherry in the centre, and cutting eight strips of green angelica like spikes, reaching from the cherry to the edge of the pine-apple. They should be cut in exact lengths, so as not to overlap. The top of the pine-apple looks like a green star with a red centre.

Pears, Tinned.—Tinned pears are exceedingly nice in flavour, but the drawback to them is their appearance. They look like pale and rather dirty wax, while the syrup with which they are surrounded resembles the water in which potatoes have been over-boiled. The prettiest way of sending them to table is as follows:—Take, say a teacupful of rice, wash it very carefully, boil it, and let it get dry and cold. Take the syrup from the pears and taste it, and if not sweet enough add some powdered sugar. Put the rice in a glass dish, and make a very small well in the centre, and pour all the syrup into this, so that it soaks into the rice at the bottom of the dish without affecting the appearance of the surface. In the meantime, place the pears themselves on a dish, and let the syrup drain off them, and if you can let them stand for an hour or two to let them dry all the better. Now, with an ordinary brush, paint these waxy-looking pears a bright red with a little cochineal, and place these half-pears on the white rice, slanting, with the thick part downwards and the stalk end uppermost. Cut a few sticks of green angelica about an inch and a half long and of the thickness of the ordinary stalk of a pear, and stick one of these into the stalk end of each pear. The red pear, with the green stalk resting on the snow-white bed of rice, looks very pretty. A little chopped angelica can be sprinkled over the white rice, like chopped parsley.

Fruits, Bottled.—When apricots and peaches are preserved in bottles, they can be treated exactly in a similar manner to those preserved in tins. It will be found advisable, however, to taste the syrup in the bottle, as it will be often found that it requires the addition of a little more sugar. Ordinary bottled fruits, such as gooseberries, currants, raspberries, rhubarb, damsons, cranberries, etc., can be used for making fruit pies, or they can be sent to table simply as stewed fruit. In this case some whipped cream on the top is a very great improvement. Another very nice way of sending these bottled fruits to table is to fill a border made with rice, as described in Chapter III.

CHAPTER X.

JELLIES (VEGETARIAN) AND JAMS.

By vegetarian jelly we mean jellies made on vegetarian principles. To be consistent, if we cannot use anchovy sauce because it is made from fish, on the same principle we cannot use either gelatine or isinglass, which, of course, as everybody knows, is made from fishes. For all this, there is no reason why vegetarians should not enjoy jellies quite equal, so far as flavour is concerned, to ordinary jelly. The simplest substitute for gelatine, or what is virtually the same thing, isinglass, is corn-flour. Tapioca could be used, but corn-flour saves much trouble. Some persons may urge that it is not fair to give the name of jelly to a corn-flour pudding. There is, however, a very great difference between a corn-flour pudding flavoured with orange, and what we may call an orange jelly, in which corn-flour is only introduced, like gelatine, for the purpose of transforming a liquid into a solid.

We also have this advantage in using corn-flour : it is much more simple and can be utilised for making a very large variety of jellies, many of which, probably, will be new even to vegetarians themselves. We are all agreed on one point, *i.e.*, the wholesomeness of freshly picked ripe fruit. We will suppose the season to be autumn and the blackberries ripe on the hedgerows, and that the children of the family are nothing loth to gather, say, a couple of quarts. We will now describe how to make a mould of—

Blackberry Jelly.—Put the blackberries in an enamelled saucepan with a little water at the bottom, and let them stew gently till they yield up their juice, or they can be placed in a jar in the oven. They can now be strained through a hair sieve, but, still better, they can be squeezed dry in a tamis cloth. This juice should now be sweetened, and it can be made into jelly in two ways, both of which are perfectly lawful in vegetarian cookery. The juice, like red currant juice, can be boiled with a large quantity of white sugar till the jelly sets of its own accord; in this case we should require one pound of sugar to every pint of juice, and the result would be a blackberry jelly like red currant jelly, more like a preserve than the jelly we are accustomed to eat at dinner alone. For instance, no one would care to eat a quantity of red currant jelly like we should ordinary orange or lemon jelly—it would be too sickly; consequently we will take a pint or a quart of our blackberry juice only and sufficient sugar to make it agreeably sweet without being sickly. We will boil this in a saucepan and add a tablespoonful of corn-flour mixed with a little cold juice to every pint to make the juice thick. This can be now poured into a mould or plain round basin; we will suppose the latter. When the jelly has got quite cold we can turn it out on to a dish, say a silver dish, with a piece of white ornamental paper at the bottom. We now have to ornament this mould of blackberry jelly, and, as a rule, it will be found that no ornament can surpass natural ones. Before boiling the blackberries for the purpose of extracting their juice, pick out two or three dozen of the largest and ripest, wash them and put them by with some of the young green leaves of the blackberry plant itself, which should be picked as nearly as possible of the same size, and, like the blackberries, must be washed. Now place a row of blackberry leaves round the base of the mould, with the stalk of the leaf under the mould, and on each leaf place a ripe blackberry touching the mould itself. Take four very small leaves and stick them on the top of the mould, in the centre, and put the largest and best-looking blackberry of all upright in the centre. This dish is now pretty-looking enough to be served on really great occasions. We consider this dish worthy of being called blackberry jelly, and not corn-flour pudding.

Lemon Jelly.—Take six lemons and half a pound of sugar, and rub the sugar on the outside of three of the lemons; the lemons must be hard and yellow, the peel should not be shrivelled. Now squeeze the juice of all six lemons into a basin, add the sugar and a pint of water. Of course, the lemon-juice must be strained. (If wine is allowed, add half a pint of good golden sherry or Madeira.) Bring this to the boil and thicken it with some corn-flour in the ordinary way, allowing a tablespoonful of corn-flour for every pint of fluid. Pour it into a mould and when it is set turn it out. A lemon jelly like this should be turned on to a piece of ornamental paper placed at the bottom of a silver or some other kind of dish. The base of the mould should be ornamented with thin slices of lemon cut in half, the diameter touching the base of the mould and the semicircular piece of peel outside. If a round basin has been used for a mould, place a corner of a lemon on the top in the middle, surrounded with a few imitation green leaves cut out of angelica. This improves the dish in appearance and also shows what the dish is made of.

Orange Jelly.—Take six oranges, two lemons, and half a pound of lump sugar; rub the sugar on the outside of three of the oranges, squeeze the juice of the six oranges into a basin with the juice of two lemons, strain, add the sugar and a pint of water. The liquid will be of an orange colour, owing to the rind of the orange rubbed on to the sugar. (If wine be allowed, add half a pint of golden sherry or Madeira.) Bring the liquid to boiling point and then thicken it with corn-flour, and pour it while hot into a mould or plain white basin; when cold, turn it out on to a piece of ornamental paper placed at the bottom of a dish; surround the bottom of the mould with thin slices of orange cut into quarters and the centre part pushed under the mould; place the small end of an orange on the top of the mould with some little leaves or spikes of green angelica placed round the edge.

Black Currant Jelly.—The juice of black currants makes excellent jelly in the ordinary way if we boil a pint of black currant juice with a pound of sugar till it sets; but a mould of black currant jelly suitable to be used as a sweet at dinner can be made by adding less sugar and thickening the juice with corn-flour, allowing about a tablespoonful to every pint, and pouring it into a mould or plain round basin. The mould can be ornamented as follows, and we will suppose a pudding-basin to be used for the purpose. We will suppose the mould of jelly to have been turned out on to a clean sheet of white paper. Pick some of the brighter green black-currant leaves off the tree, and place these round the base of the mould with the stalk of the leaf pushed underneath and the point of the leaf pointing outwards. Now choose a few very small bunches of black currants, wash these and dip them into very weak gum and water, and then dip them into white powdered sugar. They now look, when they are dry, as if they were crystallised or covered with hoar-frost. Place one of these little bunches, with the stalk stuck into the mould of jelly, about an inch from the bottom, so that each bunch rests on a green leaf. Cut a small stick of angelica and stick it into the top of the mould upright, and let a bunch of frosted black currants hang over the top. If we wish to make the mould of jelly very pretty as a supper dish, where there is a good top light, we can dip the green leaves into weak gum and water and then sprinkle over them some powdered glass.

Red Currant Jelly.—Red currant jelly can be made in exactly a similar manner, substituting red currants for black.

Raspberry Jelly.—The raspberries should be picked very ripe, and two or three dozen of the best-looking ones of the largest and ripest should be reserved for ornamenting. If possible, also gather some red currants and mix with the raspberries, on account of the colour, which otherwise would be very poor indeed. It will be found best to rub the raspberries through a hair sieve, as the addition of the pulp very much improves the flavour of the jelly. The sieve should be sufficiently fine to prevent the pips of the raspberries passing through it. The juice and pulp from the raspberries and currants can now be thickened with corn-flour as directed in the recipe for blackberry jelly. Raspberry leaves should be placed round the base of the jelly and a ripe raspberry placed on each. The best-looking raspberry can be placed on the top of the mould in the centre of two or three raspberry leaves stuck in the jelly.

Apple Jam and Apple Jelly.—The following recipe is taken from "A Year's Cookery," by Phyllis Browne:—"The best time for making apple jelly is about the middle of November. Almost all kinds of apples may be used for the purpose, though, if a clear white jelly is wanted, Colvilles or orange-pippins should be chosen; if red jelly is preferred, very rosy-cheeked apples should be taken, and the skins should be boiled with the fruit. Apple jam is made of the fruit after the juice has been drawn off for jelly. Economical housekeepers will find that very excellent jelly can be made of apple parings, so that where apples in any quantity have been used for pies and tarts the skins can be stewed in sufficient water to cover them, and when the liquor is strongly flavoured it can be strained and boiled with sugar to a jelly. To make apple jelly, pare, core and slice the apples and put them into a preserving-pan with enough water to cover them. Stir them occasionally and stew gently till the apples have fallen, then turn all into a jelly-bag and strain away the juice, but do not squeeze or press the pulp. Measure the liquid and allow a pound of sugar to a pint of juice. Put both juice and sugar back into the preserving-pan, and, if liked, add one or two cloves tied in muslin, or two or three inches of lemon-rind. Boil gently and skim carefully for about half an hour, or till a little of the jelly put upon a plate will set. Pour it while hot into jars, and when cold and stiff cover down in the usual way. If yellow jelly is wanted a pinch of saffron tied in muslin should be boiled with the juice. To make apple jam, weigh the apple pulp after the juice has been drawn from it, rub it through a hair sieve, and allow one pound of sugar to one pint of pulp, and the grated rind of a lemon to three pints of pulp. Boil all gently together till the jam will set when a little is put on a plate. Apple jam is sometimes flavoured with vanilla instead of lemon."

Damson Jelly.—Damson jelly can be made in two ways. The juice can be boiled with sugar till it gets like red currant jelly, or the juice of the damsons can be sweetened with less sugar and thickened with corn-flour. In order to extract the juice from damsons they should be sliced and placed in a jar or basin and put in the oven. They are best left in the oven all night. If the mould of jelly is made in a round basin, a single whole damson can be placed on the top of the mould and green leaves placed round the base.

Pine-apple Jelly.—The syrup from a preserved pine, should the pine-apple itself be used for mixing with other fruits, or for ornamental purposes, can be utilised by being made into a mould of jelly and by being thickened with cornflour. It will bear the addition of a little water.

Apricot Jelly.—The juice from tinned apricots can be treated like that of pine-apple. When a mixture of fruits is served in a large bowl, the syrup from tinned fruits should not be added, but at the same time, of course, should be used in some other way.

Mulberry Jelly.—Mulberries, of course, would not be bought for the purpose, but those who possess a mulberry tree in their garden will do well to utilise what are called windfalls by making mulberry jelly. The juice can be extracted by placing the fruit in a jar and putting it in the oven; sugar must be added, and the juice thickened with corn-flour. There are few other ways of using unripe mulberries.

Jams.—Home-made jam is not so common now as it was some years back. As a rule, it does not answer from an economical point of view to *buy* fruit to make jam. On the other hand, those who possess a garden will find home-made jam a great saving. Those who have attempted to sell their fruit probably know this to their cost. In making every kind of jam it is essential the fruit should be picked dry. It is also a time-honoured tradition that the fruit is best picked when basking in the morning sun. It is also necessary that the fruit should be free from dust, and that all decayed or rotten fruit should be carefully picked out.

Jam is made by boiling the fruit with sugar, and it is false economy to get common sugar; cheap sugar throws up a quantity of scum. Years back many persons used brown sugar, but in the present day the difference in the price of brown and white sugar is so trifling that the latter should always be used for the purpose. The sugar should not be crushed. It is best to boil the fruit before adding the sugar. The scum should be removed, and a wooden spoon used for the purpose. A large enamel stew-pan can be used, but tradition is in favour of a brass preserving-pan. It will be found best to boil the fruit as rapidly as possible. The quantity of sugar varies slightly with the fruit used. Supposing we have a pound of fruit, the following list gives what is generally considered about the proper quantity of sugar:—

APRICOT JAM.—Three-quarters of a pound.

BLACKBERRY JAM.—Half a pound; if apple is mixed, rather more.

BLACK CURRANT JAM.—One pound.

RED CURRANT JAM.—One pound.

DAMSON JAM.—One pound.

GOOSEBERRY JAM.—Three-quarters of a pound.

GREENGAGE JAM.—Three-quarters of a pound.

PLUM JAM.—One pound.

RASPBERRY JAM.—One pound.

STRAWBERRY JAM.—Three-quarters of a pound.

CARROT JAM.—If you wish the jam to be of a good colour, only use the outside or red part of the carrots. Add the rind and the juice of one lemon, and one pound of sugar to every pound of pulp; a little brandy is a great improvement.

RHUBARB JAM.—To every pound of pulp add three-quarters of a pound of sugar, and the juice of one lemon and the rind of half a lemon. Essence of almonds can be substituted for the lemon.

VEGETABLE MARROW JAM.—Add three-quarters of a pound of sugar to every pound of pulp. The jam can be flavoured either with ginger or lemon-juice.

CHAPTER XI.

CREAMS, CUSTARDS, AND CHEESE-CAKES.

Creams.—Creams may be divided into two classes— whipped cream, flavoured in a variety of ways, and the solid moulds of cream, which when turned out look extremely elegant, but which when tasted are somewhat disappointing. These latter moulds owe their firmness and consistency to the addition of isinglass, and, as this substance is not allowed in vegetarian cookery, we shall be able to dispense with cream served in this form, nor are we losers by so doing. The ordinary mould of cream is too apt to taste like spongy liver, and, so far as palate is concerned, is incomparably inferior to the more delicate whipped creams. Just in the same way a good rich custard made with yolks of eggs is spoilt by being turned into a solid custard by the addition of gelatine. In order to have good whipped cream, the first essential is to obtain pure cream. This greatly depends upon the neighbourhood in which we live. In country houses, away from large towns, there is as a rule no trouble, whereas in London really good cream can only be obtained with great difficulty. There is a well-known old story of the London milkman telling the cook who complained of the quality of the cream to stir it up, as the cream settled at the bottom. We will not enter into the subject of the adulteration of cream in big cities, as probably many of these stories are gross exaggerations, though it is said that pigs' brains and even horses' brains have been used for the purpose of giving the cream a consistency, while undoubtedly turmeric has been used to give it a colour.

We will suppose that we have, say, a quart of really good thick cream. All that is necessary is to beat up the cream with a whisk till it becomes a froth. This is much more easily done in cold weather than in hot, and, if the weather be very warm, it is best to put the tin or pan containing the cream into ice an hour or two before it is used. Old French cookery-books recommend the addition of a little powdered gum, not bigger than a pea, and the gum recommended is that known as tragacanth. Others again beat up the white of an egg to a stiff froth, and add this to the cream. It is a good plan when the cream fails to froth completely to take off the top froth and drain it on a sieve placed upside down. The cream that drains through can be added to what is left and re-whipped. It is also a good plan to make whipped cream some time before it is wanted, and, indeed, it can be prepared with advantage the day before. When the cream is drained (we are supposing a quart to have been used) it should be mixed with three or four ounces of very finely powdered sugar, as well as the particular kind of flavouring that will give the cream its name. For instance, we can have, if liqueurs are allowed—

Maraschino Cream.—This is simply made by mixing a small glass of maraschino with some whipped cream, properly sweetened.

Coffee Cream.—Make a very strong infusion of pure coffee that has been roasted a high colour. It will be found best to re-roast coffee berries in the oven if you have not got a proper coffee-roaster. Pound the berries in a pestle and mortar, or grind them very coarsely; then make a strong infusion with a very small quantity of water, and strain it till it is quite bright. This is mixed with the whipped sweetened cream.

Chocolate Cream.—Take about two ounces of the very best chocolate and dissolve it in a little boiling water; let it get cold, and then mix with the whipped sweetened cream.

Vanilla Cream.—Vanilla cream is nicest when a fresh vanilla pod is used for the purpose, but a more simple process is to use a little essence of vanilla.

Orange Cream.—Rub some lumps of sugar on the outside of an orange, and pound this sugar very finely, and then mix it with the whipped cream.

Lemon Cream.—Proceed exactly as in making orange cream, only substituting lemon for orange.

Strawberry Cream.—The juice only of the strawberry should be used. This juice should be mixed with the powdered sugar and then used for mixing with the whipped cream. It is a mistake, in making creams, to have too much flavouring. The juice of a quarter of a pound of ripe red strawberries would be sufficient for a quart of cream.

Pistachio Cream.—Take about half a pound of pistachio kernels, throw them for a minute or two into boiling water, and then rub off the skins, throwing them into cold water like you do in blanching almonds. Pound these in a mortar with a tablespoonful of orange-flower water, and mix a little spinach extract to give it a colour. Now mix this with the whipped sweetened cream very thoroughly. This bright green cream makes a very elegant dish.

Custards.—Good custard forms, perhaps, the best cold sweet sauce known. It can be made very cheaply, and, on the other hand, it may be made in such a manner as to be very expensive. We will first describe how to make the most expensive kind of custard, as very often we can gather ideas from a high-class model and carry them out in an inexpensive way. The highest class custard is made by only using yolks of eggs instead of whole eggs, and we can use cream in addition to milk. The great art in making custard is to take care it does not curdle. Six yolks of eggs, half a pint of milk, half a pint of cream, sweetened, would, of course, form a very expensive custard. An ordinary custard can be made as follows:—Take four large or five small eggs, beat them up very thoroughly, and add them gradually to a pint of sweetened milk that has been boiled separately. In order to thicken the custard, it is a good plan to put it in a jug and stand the jug in a saucepan of boiling water, and stir the custard till it is sufficiently thick. Custard can be flavoured in various ways. One of the cheapest and perhaps nicest is to boil one or two bay-leaves in the milk. Custard can also be flavoured by the addition of a small quantity of the essence of vanilla; if you use a fresh pod vanilla, tie it up in a little piece of muslin and have a string to it. This can be boiled in the milk till the milk is sufficiently flavoured, and this pod can be used over and over again. Of course, as it loses its flavour, it will have to remain in the milk longer.

Cheap Custard.—A very cheap custard can be made by adding to one pint of boiled milk one well-beaten-up egg and one good-sized teaspoonful of corn-flour. The milk should be first sweetened, and can be flavoured very cheaply by rubbing a few lumps of sugar on the outside of a lemon, or by having a few bay-leaves boiled in it. A rich yellow colour can be obtained by using a small quantity of yellow vegetable colouring extract, which, like the green colouring, is sold in bottles by all grocers. These bottles are very cheap, as they last a long time. They simply give any kind of pudding a rich colouring without imparting any flavour whatever, and in this respect are very superior to saffron.

Apple Custard.—Good apple custard can only be made by using apples of a good flavour. When apples are in season, this dish can be made fairly cheaply, but it does not do to use those high-priced imported apples. Peel and take out the cores of about four pounds of apples, and let these simmer till they are quite tender in rather more than a pint of water. Add about one pound of sugar, or rather less if the apples are sweet; add a little powdered cinnamon, and mix all this with eight eggs, well beaten up; stir the mixture very carefully in a saucepan, or better still in a good-sized jug placed in a saucepan, till it begins to thicken. This custard is best served in glasses, and a little cinnamon sugar can be shaken over the top. Nutmeg may be used instead of cinnamon, and by many is thought superior.

Cheese-cakes.—Cheese-cakes can be sent to table in two forms, the one some rich kind of custard or cream placed in little round pieces of pastry, or we can have a so-called cheese-cake baked in a pie-dish, the edges only of which are lined with puff paste. We can also have cheese-cakes very rich and cheese-cakes very plain. The origin of the name cheese-cake is that originally they were made from curds used in making cheese. Probably most people consider that the cheese-cakes made from curds are superior, and in the North of England, and especially in Yorkshire, where curds are exposed for sale in the windows at so much a pound, very delicious cheese-cakes can be made, but considerable difficulty will be experienced if we attempt to make home-made curds from London milk. Curds are made by taking any quantity of milk and letting it nearly boil, then throw in a little rennet or a glass of sherry. The curds must be well strained.

Cheese-cakes from Curds.—Take half a pound of curds and press the curds in a napkin to extract the moisture. Take also six ounces of lump sugar, and rub the sugar on the outside of a couple of oranges or lemons. Dissolve this sugar in two ounces of butter made hot in a tin in the oven; mix this with the curds, with two ounces of powdered ratafias and a little grated nutmeg—about half a nutmeg to this quantity will be required; add also six yolks of eggs. Mix this well together, and fill the tartlet cases, made from puff paste, and bake them in the oven. It is often customary to place in the centre of each cheese-cake a thin strip of candied peel. As soon as the cheese-cakes are done, take them out of the oven, and if the mixture be of a bad colour finish it off with a salamander, but do not let them remain in the oven too long, so that the pastry becomes brittle and dried up. These cheese-cakes can be made on a larger scale than the ordinary one so familiar to all who have looked into a pastry-cook's window. Suppose we make them of the size of a breakfast saucer, a very rich and delicious cheese-cake can be made by adding some chopped dried cherries to the mixture. Sometimes ordinary grocer's currants are added and the ratafias omitted. Sultana raisins can be used instead of currants, and by many are much preferred.

This mixture can be baked in a shallow pie-dish and the edge of the dish lined with puff paste, but cheese-cakes made from curds are undoubtedly expensive.

Cheese-cakes from Potatoes.—Exceedingly nice cheese-cakes can be made from remains of cold potatoes, and can be made very cheap by increasing the quantity of potatoes used. Take a quarter of a pound of butter, four eggs, two fresh lemons, and half a pound of lump sugar. First of all rub off all the outsides of two lemons on to the sugar; oil the butter in a tin in the oven and melt the sugar in it; squeeze the juice of the two lemons, and take care that the sugar is thoroughly dissolved before you begin to mix all the ingredients together. Now beat up the eggs very thoroughly and mix the whole in a basin. This now forms a very rich mixture indeed, a good-sized teaspoonful of which would be sufficient for the interior of an ordinary-sized cheese-cake, but a far better plan is to make a large cheese-cake, or rather cheese-cake pudding, in a pie-dish by adding cold boiled potatoes. The plainness or richness of the pudding depends entirely upon the amount of potatoes added. The pie-dish can be lined with a little puff paste round the edge, if preferred, or the pudding can be sent to table plain. It should be baked in the oven till the top is nicely browned. It can be served either hot or cold, but, in our opinion, is nicer cold. If the lemons are very fresh and green—if the pudding is sent to table *hot*—you will often detect the smell of turpentine. If a *large* quantity of potatoes is added more sugar will be required.

Orange Cheese-cake.—Proceed exactly as above, only substituting two oranges for two lemons.

Almond Cheese-cakes.—Proceed exactly as above, only instead of rubbing the sugar on the outside of lemons add a small quantity of essence of almonds.

Apple Cheese-cakes.—Apple cheese-cakes can be made in a similar manner to apple custard, the only difference being that the mixture is baked till it sets.

CHAPTER XII.

STEWED FRUITS AND FRUIT ICES.

THERE are few articles of diet more wholesome than fruit, in every shape, provided it is *fresh*. It is a great mistake, however, to suppose that fruit, when too stale to be eaten as it is, is yet good enough for stewing. We often hear, especially in summer weather, of persons being made ill from eating fruit. Probably in every case the injury results, not from eating fruit as fruit, but from eating it when it is too stale to be served as an article of food at all. There is an immense amount of injury done to this country by the importation of rotten plums, more especially from Germany, and it is to be regretted that more stringent laws are not made to prevent the importation of all kinds of food hurtful to health.

We will suppose that in every recipe we are about to give the fruit is at any rate fresh; we do not say ripe, because there are many instances in which fruit not ripe enough to be eaten raw is exceedingly wholesome when stewed properly and sweetened. As an instance we may mention green gooseberries and hard greengages, which, though quite uneatable in their natural state, yet make delicious fruit pies or dishes of stewed fruit. Of all dishes there are few to equal what is called a compote of fruit, and there are probably few sweets more popular than—

Compote of Fruit.—A compote of fruit consists of a variety of fresh fruits mixed together in a bowl. Some may be stewed and some served in their natural state, or the whole may be stewed. When a large variety of fruits can be obtained, and are sent to table in an old-fashioned china family bowl, few dishes present a more elegant appearance, especially if you happen to possess an old-fashioned punch ladle, an old silver bowl with a black whalebone handle. Care should be taken to keep the fruit from being broken. The following fruits will mix very well, although, of course, it is impossible always to obtain every variety. We can have strawberries, raspberries, red, white, and black currants, and cherries, as well as peaches, nectarines, and apricots. We can also have stewed apples and stewed pears. Very much, of course, will depend upon the time of year. Those fruits that want stewing should be placed in some hot syrup previously made, and only allowed to stew till tender enough to be eaten. Tinned fruits, especially apricots, can be mixed with fresh fruits, only it is best not to use the syrup in the tin, as it will probably overpower the flavour of the other fruits. The syrup, as far as possible, should be bright and not cloudy. The fruit in the bowl should be mixed, but should not be stirred up. We should endeavour as much as possible to keep the colours distinct. If strawberries or raspberries form part of the compote, the syrup will get red. Should black currants be present, avoid breaking them, as they spoil the appearance of the syrup. In summer the compote of fruits is much improved by the addition of a lump of ice and a glass of good old brandy. Should the compote of fruits, as is often the case, be intended for a garden party, where it will have to stand a long time, if possible get a small bowl, like those in which gold and silver fish are sold in the street for sixpence, and fill this with ice and place it in the middle of the larger bowl containing fruit, otherwise the melted ice will utterly spoil the juice that runs from the fruit, which is sweetened with the syrup and flavoured with the brandy. If much brandy be added, old ladies at garden parties will be found to observe that the juice is the best part of it.

Apples, Stewed.—Peel and cut out the cores of the apples, and stew them gently in some syrup composed of about half a pound of white sugar and rather more than a pint of water. A small stick of cinnamon, or a few cloves, and a strip of lemon-peel can be added to the syrup, but should be taken out when finished. The apples should be stewed till they are tender, but must not be broken. The syrup in which the apples are stewed should of course be served with them. This syrup can be coloured slightly with a few drops of cochineal, but should not be coloured more than very slightly. The syrup looks a great deal better if it is clear and bright. It can be strained and clarified. Apples are very nice stewed in white French wine, such as Chablis or Graves.

Stewed Pears.—Pears known as cooking pears take a long time to stew. They should be peeled and the cores removed, and then stewed very gently in a syrup composed of half a pound of sugar to about a pint and a half of water; add a few cloves to the syrup, say two cloves to each pear. The pears will probably take from two to three hours to stew before they are tender. When tender add a glass of port wine and a little cochineal. If the pears are stewed, like they are abroad, in claret, add cinnamon instead of the cloves.

Stewed Rhubarb.—Stewed rhubarb is of two kinds. When it first comes into season it is small, tender, and of a bright red colour, and when stewed makes a very pretty dish. The red rhubarb should be cut into little pieces about two inches long. Very little water will be required, as the fruit contains a great deal of water in itself. The amount of sugar added depends entirely upon taste. The stewed rhubarb should be sent to table unbroken, and floating in a bright red juice.

When rhubarb is old and green it is best served more like a purée, or mashed. Very old rhubarb is often stringy, and can with advantage be rubbed through a wire sieve. It is no use attempting to colour old rhubarb red, but you can improve its colour by the addition of a very little spinach extract. A few strips of lemon-peel can be stewed with old rhubarb, but should never be added to young red rhubarb.

Gooseberries, Stewed.—Young green gooseberries stewed, strange to say, require less sugar than ripe gooseberries. It is best to stew the fruit first, and add the sugar afterwards. The amount of sugar varies very much with the quality of the gooseberries.

Prunes, Stewed.—The prunes should be washed before they are stewed. They will not take more than half an hour to stew, and a strip of lemon-peel should be placed in the juice. Stewed prunes are much improved by the addition of a little port wine.

Plums, Stewed.—Stewed plums, such as black, ordinary, or greengages, or indeed any kind of stone fruit, can be stewed in syrup, and have this advantage—plums can be used this way which could not be eaten at all if they were raw. These fruits are much nicer cold than hot. In many cases, in stewing stone fruit (and this applies particularly to peaches, apricots, and nectarines), the stones should be removed and cracked and the kernels added to the fruit.

Cherries, Stewed.—Large white-heart cherries form a very delicate dish when stewed. Very little water should be added, and the syrup should be kept as white as possible, and, if necessary, strained. Stew the cherries till they are tender, but do not let them break. Colour the syrup with a few drops of cochineal, and add a glass of maraschino.

Ices.—Ices are too often regarded as expensive luxuries, and show how completely custom rules the majority of our housekeepers. There are many houses where the dinner may consist daily of soup, fish, entrées, joint, game, and wine, and yet, were we to suggest a course of ices, the worthy housekeeper would hesitate on the ground of extravagance. It is difficult to argue with persons whose definition of economy is what they have always been accustomed to since they were children, and whose definition of extravagance is anything new. The fact remains, however, that there is many a worthy signor who sells ices in the streets at a penny each, and manages to make a living out of the profit not only for himself, but for his signora as well. Under these circumstances, the manufacture of these "extravagances" is worthy of inquiry. Ices can be made at home very cheaply with an ice machine, which can now be obtained at a, comparatively speaking, small cost. With a machine there is absolutely no trouble, and directions will be given with each machine, so that any details here, which vary with the machine, will be useless. Ices can be made at home without a machine with a little trouble, and, to explain how to do this, it is necessary to explain the theory of ice-making, which is exceedingly simple. We will not allude to machines dependent on freezing-powders, but to those which rely for their cold simply on ice and salt mixed. We will suppose we want a lemon-water ice, *i.e.*, we have made some very strong and sweet lemonade, and we want to freeze it. It is well known that water will freeze at a certain temperature, called freezing-point. By mixing chopped ice and salt and a very little water together, a far greater degree of cold can be immediately produced, viz., a thermometer would stand at 32° below freezing-point were it to be plunged into this mixture. An ice machine is a metal pail placed in another pail much larger than itself. The "sweet lemonade" is placed in the middle pail, and chopped ice and salt placed outside it. The proportion of ice to salt should be double the weight of the former to the latter. It is now obvious that if we have filled two pails, the one with "the sweet lemonade," and the other with the ice and salt, very soon our lemonade will be a solid block of ice. To prevent this it must be constantly stirred, and, as the lemonade would of course freeze first against the sides of the pail, these sides must be constantly scraped. Inside the inner pail, consequently, there is a stirrer, which, by means of a handle, continually scrapes the side of the pail. It is obvious that if the stirrer is fixed, and the pail itself made to revolve, that is the same as if the pail were fixed and the stirrer made to revolve. To make lemon-water ice, therefore, place the lemonade in the inner pail, surrounded with chopped ice and salt, two parts of the former to one of the latter, turn the handle, and in a few minutes the ice is made. Now, suppose you have not got a machine, proceed as follows: Take an empty, clean, round coffee-tin (the larger the better). [We mention coffee-tin as the most probable one to be in the house, but any round tin will do.] Get a clean piece of wood, the same width as the inside diameter of the tin, only it must be a great deal longer. We will suppose the tin rather more than a foot deep and five inches in diameter. Our piece of wood, which should be clean and smooth, must be nearly five inches wide, say a quarter of an inch thick, and about two feet long. Next get a small tub, say nine inches deep, place the round tin in the middle, with the sweet lemonade inside; next place the piece of wood upright in the tin, so that the wood touches the bottom. Next surround the tin with chopped ice and salt up to the edge of the tub, fill it as high as you can, and then cover it round with a blanket, i.e., cover the ice and salt. Now get someone to hold the wooden board steady;

take the tin in your two hands, and turn it round and round, first one way and then another. In a very short time you will find the tin to contain lemon-water ice. The following hints, rather than recipes, for making ices, *i.e.*, for making the liquid, which must be frozen as directed above, are given not because they are the best recipes, but because cream, which is the basis of all first-class ices, is often too expensive to be used constantly. Of course, real cream is far superior to any substitute.

Ice Cream, Cheap.—Make a custard (*see* CUSTARD) with half a pint of milk, the yolks of two eggs, and a tablespoonful of Swiss milk and some sugar. As soon as it gets a little thick, stir it till it is nearly cold, then add some essence of vanilla or almonds, or a wineglassful of noyeau, or any flavouring wished, and freeze.

Ices from Fresh Fruits.—Take half a pound of fresh strawberries or raspberries, add half that weight of sugar, pound thoroughly, rub through a sieve, and mix with this thick juice, rubbed through, half a pint of the mixture made for ice cream (*see* ICE CREAM, CHEAP), only, of course, without any flavouring such as vanilla, etc. Mix thoroughly, and freeze.

N.B.—A few red currants should be mixed with the raspberries. Should the colour be poor, brighten it up before freezing with a little cochineal.

Ices from Jam.—Mix a quarter of a pound of any jam with half a pint of the mixture made for ice cream (*see* ICE CREAM, CHEAP), without any flavouring such as vanilla. Rub all through a fine sieve, and freeze. Cochineal will give additional colour to red jams; spinach extract to green jams; and a very little turmeric, or yellow vegetable colouring, to yellow jams. A small pinch of turmeric can be boiled in the milk.

Ice, Lemon-Water.—Rub six lumps of sugar on the rind of six lemons, add this and the juice of six lemons to a pint of fairly sweet syrup. The amount of sugar is a matter of taste. Strain and freeze. Some persons add a few drops of dilute sulphuric acid.

Ice, Orange-Water.—Act exactly as in lemon-water,

using oranges instead of lemons, and syrup containing less sugar.

Ice, Water Fruit.—All sorts of water fruit ices can be made by mixing half a pint of juice, such as currant-juice, with twice that quantity of syrup, and freezing. Grated ripe pineapple, pounded and bruised, ripe cherries and greengages, strawberry-juice, raspberry-juice, can be mixed with syrup and frozen. Sometimes a little lemon-juice can be added with advantage, and in the case of cherry ice and greengage ice a little noyeau added is an improvement.

CHAPTER XIII.

CAKES AND BREAD.

IN vegetarian cookery there is no difference, as far as cake-making is concerned, between it and ordinary cookery. In making cakes we will confine our attention chiefly to general principles which, if once known, render cake-making of every description comparatively easy work. Those who wish for detailed *recipes* for making almost every kind of cake known will find all that they require on a large scale in "Cassell's Dictionary of Cookery," and also everything necessary on a smaller scale in "Cassell's Shilling Cookery," which has already reached its hundred-thousandth edition.

Cakes may be divided into two classes—those that contain fruit and those that do not. Plum cakes can be made very rich indeed, like a wedding cake, or so plain that it can scarcely be distinguished from a loaf of bread with a few currants in it. Again, cakes that contain no fruit can, at the same time, be made exceedingly rich, the richness chiefly depending upon the amount of butter and eggs that are used. We will first give a few directions with regard to making what may be termed plain cakes, *i.e.*, cakes that contain no fruit at all. Perhaps the best model we can give to illustrate the general principles will be that of a pound cake. The recipe is a very easy one to recollect, as a pound cake means one that is made from a pound of butter, a pound of sugar, a pound of eggs, and a pound of flour. There is one addition, however, which the good plain cook will probably not be up to, and which, so far as flavour is concerned, makes all the difference between Francatelli and "Jemima Ann"—we must rub some of the lumps of sugar on the outsides of either two oranges or two lemons. It is also a great improvement to add a small glass of brandy, and in every kind of cake we must add a pinch of salt.

In making cakes it is always necessary to be careful about the butter. It is best to put the butter in cold water before it is used, and, if salt butter, it should be washed in several waters to extract the salt. The next thing necessary is to beat the butter to a cream. To do this it must be worked about in a basin with a wooden spoon. The basin should be a strong one, and a wooden spoon is far preferable to a metal one. You simply beat the butter and spread it against the sides of the basin and knock it about till it loses its consistency. You cannot beat the butter to the consistency of ordinary cream, but to a state more resembling Devonshire clotted cream. Of course, when it is like this it is much more easily mixed with the other ingredients. In making a pound cake we should first of all beat the butter to a cream and then add flour, sugar, and eggs gradually. When the whole is thoroughly well mixed together, we must bake it in a tin, or mould, or hoop. We need say nothing about tins or moulds, but will confine ourselves to giving directions how to bake a cake in a hoop, for, as a rule, ordinary English cooks do not understand how to use them.

One great advantage of using a hoop is that when the cake is baked there is no fear of breaking it in turning it out. A very simple hoop can be made with an ordinary slip of tin, say six inches wide; as the tin will lap over, the cake can be made any size round you wish. It is a good plan to fasten a piece of copper wire round the outside of the tin. This can be twisted, and when the cake is baked and has got cold can be untwisted, and the tin will then open of its own accord. The tin must be lined with buttered paper, and buttered paper must be placed on a flat piece of tin at the bottom. When an "amateur hoop" is used like we have described, care must be taken that the cake does not come out at the bottom. The cake, especially when it is made with beaten-up eggs, like sponge cake, will rise, and unless precautions are taken the tin will rise with it, and the unset portion of the cake break loose round the edge at the bottom. To prevent this the tin must be kept down with a weight at the top. In a proper hoop made for the purpose there are appliances for fastening the hoop together itself and also for keeping it in its place, but if we use a strip of tin we must place something across the tin on the top and then put on a heavy weight. When this is done, you must remember to allow room for the cake to rise. A pound cake such as we have described can be made into a rich fruit cake by adding stoned raisins, currants, chopped candied peel, sultana raisins, or, better still, dried cherries. In making ordinary cakes, when currants are used, they should be first washed and then dried; if you use damp currants the cake will probably be heavy.

With regard to the flour, it is cheapest in the end to use the best quality, and the flour should be dried and sifted. If you weigh the flour remember to dry and sift it before you weigh it, and not after. In using sugar get the best loaf; this should also be pounded and sifted.

In using eggs, of course each egg should be broken separately. Very often it is necessary to separate the yolks from the whites. This requires some little skill; you are less likely to break the yolk when you crack the egg boldly. Put the yolk from one half egg-shell into the other half, spilling as much of the white as you can. You will soon get the yolks separate. Next, remember before mixing the eggs to remove the thread or string from them. When the whites are beaten separately, you must whisk them till they become a solid froth; no liquid should remain at the bottom of the basin. The yolks should not be broken till they are wanted.

Lemon-peel is often used in making cakes, and in chopping it a little powdered sugar is a great assistance in preventing the peel sticking together. Remember only to use the *yellow* part, not the white. The white part gives the cake a bitter flavour.

Sometimes milk or cream is used in cake-making. If Swiss milk is used as a substitute, remember that less sugar will be required.

When pounded almonds are used for cakes, the almonds must be blanched by being thrown, first into boiling water, and then into cold water. In pounding them, add a little rose-water or orange-flower water, or the white of an egg, to prevent the almonds getting oily.

Nearly all plain cakes, where only a few eggs are used, will be made lighter by the addition of a little baking-powder. A very good baking-powder is made by mixing an ounce of tartaric acid with an ounce and a half of bicarbonate of soda, and an ounce and a half of arrowroot. The baking powder should be kept very dry.

A very nice way of making home-made cakes is to use some dough, which can be procured from the baker's. Suppose you have a quartern of dough, put it in a basin, cover it over with a cloth, and put it in front of the fire to rise, then spread it on a floured pastry-board, slice it up, and work in half a pound of fresh butter, half a pound of moist sugar, six eggs, a teaspoonful of salt, and half an ounce of caraway seeds. When all the ingredients are thoroughly mixed, place them in two or more well-buttered tins or hoops, and let them stand in front of the fire a little while before they are placed in the oven. Cakes can be flavoured with a variety of spices, such as cinnamon, mace, nutmeg, or powdered coriander seeds. These last are always used to give a special flavour to hot cross buns.

Bread.—Home-made bread is not so much used now as it was years back. Most housekeepers have found by experience that it is a waste both of time and money. There are very few houses among the middle classes which possess an oven capable of competing with any chance of success with a baker's oven. There are, however, many vegetarians who believe in what is called whole-meal bread. A good deal of the whole-meal bread sold as such has been found to be adulterated with substances very unwholesome to ordinary stomachs. We may mention saw-dust as one of the ingredients used for the purpose. Again, if you attempt to make whole-meal bread into loaves, you will find great difficulty in baking the loaves. This whole-meal is a very slow conductor of heat, and the result will probably be that the outside of the loaf will be very hard while the inside will be too underdone to be eaten. Consequently, should you wish to have home-made whole-meal bread, it is far best to bake it in the form of a tea-cake or flat-cake. We cannot do better, in conclusion, than quote what Sir Henry Thompson says on this subject:—"The following recipe," he says, "will be found successful, probably, after a trial or two, in producing excellent, light, friable, and most palatable bread : To two pounds of coarsely ground or crushed whole-meal, add half a pound of fine flour and a sufficient quantity of baking powder and salt; when these are well mixed, rub in two ounces of butter, and make into dough with half milk and water, or with all milk if preferred. Make rapidly into flat cakes like 'tea-cakes,' and bake without delay in a quick oven, leaving them afterwards to finish thoroughly at a lower temperature. The butter and milk supply fatty matters, in which the wheat is somewhat deficient; all the saline and mineral matters of the husk are retained; and thus a more nutritive form of bread cannot be made. Moreover, it retains the natural flavour of the wheat, in place of the insipidity which is characteristic of fine flour, although it is indisputable that bread produced from the latter, especially in Paris and Vienna, is unrivalled for delicacy, texture, and colour. Whole meal may be bought; but mills are now cheaply made for home use, and wheat may be ground to any degree of coarseness desired."

CHAPTER XIV.

PIES AND PUDDINGS.

IN vegetarian cookery, as a rule, pies and puddings are made in the same way as in ordinary cookery, with the exception that we cannot use lard or dripping in making our paste. Nor are we allowed to use suet in making crust for puddings. It would have been quite impossible to have given even a quarter of the recipes for the pies and puddings known, and we must refer those who wish for information on the subject to "Cassell's Shilling Cookery," where will be found a very complete list, but which would have occupied the whole of the space which we have devoted to recipes where vegetarian cookery, as a rule, *differs* from the ordinary.

We will, on the present occasion, confine our attention to the two points we have mentioned, viz., how to make pastry without lard or dripping, and pudding crust without suet. The first of these two points causes no difficulty whatever, as the best pastry, especially that known as puff paste, is invariably made with butter only as the fatty element; but there is one point we must not overlook.

Vegetarians are divided into two classes: those who use the animal products—butter, milk, cream, and eggs—and those who do not. This latter class contains, probably, the most respected members of the vegetarian body, as it will always be found that there is an involuntary homage paid by all men to consistency. How then are strict vegetarians to make pastry, butter being classed with the forbidden fruit? We fear we cannot tell them how to make good puff paste; but "Necessity is the mother of invention," and naturally olive oil must supply the place of butter.

Pastry without Butter.—We will describe how to make a small quantity, which is always best when we make experiments. Take half a pound of the best Vienna flour, and mix with it, while dry, about a salt-spoonful of baking-powder. Now add about a tablespoonful of olive oil, and work the oil and flour together with the fingers exactly as you work a small piece of butter into the flour at the commencement of making puff paste. Next add sufficient water to make the whole into an elastic paste; roll it out and let it set between two tins containing ice, similar to the method used in making high-class pastry.

We have mentioned a tablespoonful of oil, but if ice is used more oil may be added.

We all know that oil will freeze at a much lower temperature than water, consequently the minute particles of oil become partially solid. Now take the paste, roll it out, and give it three turns; roll it out again, give it three more turns, and put it back in the ice; let it stand ten minutes or a quarter of an hour, and repeat this process three times. Be careful to flour the pastry each time before it is turned. By this means we get the pastry in thin layers, with minute air bubbles between them, and this will cause the pastry to rise. If you are making a pie, roll out the pastry the last time, cover the pie, and put it in the oven immediately, while the pastry is cold. Do not let the pastry stand, unless it be in a very cold place.

This pastry we have just described, made with oil, can also be utilised for puddings, in which latter case we would recommend the addition of a little more baking-powder, and to every pound of flour add two tablespoonfuls of very fine bread-crumbs. These must be dry, and rubbed through a fine sieve.

Pastry with Butter.—Good puff paste is made by taking equal quantities of butter and flour—say a pound of each—the yolk of one egg, a pinch of salt, while the water used is acidulated with lemon-juice. For the manipulation of this pastry we must refer those who do not know how to make it to other cookery books, or to the shilling one above mentioned. In making ordinary paste we must use less butter; and when we use considerably less butter, if we wish the pastry light, we shall require baking-powder. The quantity depends very much upon the quality. Many persons make their own baking-powder, and we cannot recommend any better than the recipe given in the last chapter, viz., an ounce of tartaric acid, an ounce and a half of bicarbonate of soda, and an ounce and a half of arrowroot. A great deal, too, depends upon the quality of the flour. Vienna flour is much more expensive than ordinary flour, but incomparably superior. What limit we can assign to the quantity of butter used it is impossible to say. A quarter of a pound of butter to a pound of flour, and a teaspoonful of baking-powder, will make a fair crust. When less butter is used the result is not altogether satisfactory.

Puddings.—We next come to the very large class of puddings in which suet is used. The ordinary plum pudding is a case in point. The best substitute for suet, of course, is butter or oil; a plum pudding, however, made without suet, would undoubtedly be heavy, and, to avoid this, we must use butter, bread-crumbs, and baking-powder. It would be impossible to give any exact quantity, as so much depends upon the other ingredients. Some people use bread-crumbs only in making plum pudding, and no flour, in which case, of course, a very considerable number of eggs must be used or else the pudding will break to pieces. In the case, however, of oil being used as a substitute for butter, it is of the utmost importance that the oil be pure and fresh. We here have to overcome a deeply-rooted English prejudice. Pure oil is absolutely tasteless, and it has often been remarked by high-class authorities that really pure butter ought to be the same. We fear, however, that purity in food is the exception rather than the rule, as at no period of this country's history has the crime of adulteration been so rampant as in the present day.

Adulteration has been said to be another form of competition. Too often adulteration is a deliberate form of robbery. Steps have been taken in recent years to put a stop to this universal system of fraud, more especially in connection with butter. Were more Acts passed similar to the "Margarine Act" we believe that this country would be richer and happier, and without doubt more healthy.

In that large class of puddings known as custard pudding, cabinet pudding, there is no difference whatever in vegetarian

G *

cookery. It would be quite impossible to make any of these puddings without eggs, and when eggs are used we may take for granted that butter is allowed also.

We have, throughout, called particular attention to the importance of appearances. In the case of all puddings made with eggs and baked in a dish, it is a very great improvement to reserve one or two whites of egg, and to beat these to a stiff froth, with a little white powdered sugar. When the pudding is baked, cover it with this snow-white froth, and let it set by placing it in a slack oven for two or three minutes. Whether the pudding is served hot or cold, the result is the same. An otherwise plain and somewhat common-looking dish is transformed into an elegant one, the only extra expense being a little *trouble*.

We may sum up our instructions to cooks in the words: "Whatsoever thy hand findeth to do, do it with thy might."

INDEX.

Allemande Sauce, 44
Almond Cheesecakes, 170
  ,, Fritters, 119
  ,, Sauce, 44
  ,, Sauce, Clear, 45
  ,, Soup, 23
Apple Cheesecakes, 170
  ,, Custard, 168
  ,, Fritters, 118
  ,, Jam, 161
  ,, Jelly, 161
  ,, Sauce, 45
  ,, Soup, 24
Apples, Stewed, 172
Apricot Fritters, 119
  ,, Jam, 164
  ,, Jelly, 163
Apricots Tinned, 155
  ,, with Cream, 156
Aromatic Herbs, 32
Arrowroot Sauce, 45
Artichokes, French, 137
  ,, ,, à la Provençale, 137
  ,, ,, Boiled, 137
  ,, ,, Fried, 137
  ,, ,, Salad, 102
Artichoke, Jerusalem, 137
  ,, ,, Fried, 138
  ,, ,, Mashed, 138
  ,, ,, Sauce, 45
  ,, ,, Soup, 24
Asparagus and Eggs, 85
  ,, Boiled, 139
  ,, Salad, 101
  ,, Sauce, 45
  ,, Soup, 24
  ,, Tinned, 153
Ayoli, 115

Baking-Powder, 180
Banana Fritters, 119
Barley and Rice Porridge, 75
  ,, Soup, 25
Batter for Fritters, 116
Beans, Broad, 139
  ,, ,, à la Bourgeoise, 139
  ,, ,, à la Poulette, 139
  ,, ,, Mashed, 139
  ,, ,, Salad, 103
  ,, ,, Soup, 27
Beans, French, 139
  ,, ,, Pudding, 140
  ,, ,, Salad, 102
  ,, ,, Soup, 27
  ,, ,, Tinned, 154
Beans, Haricot, 131
  ,, ,, Salad, 103
  ,, ,, Soup, Red, 26
  ,, ,, Soup, White, 26
Beetroot Salad, 102
  ,, Soup, 26
Beurre Noir, 48
Blackberry Jam, 164
  ,, Jelly, 158
Black Butter, 48
  ,, ,, and Eggs, 86
Black Currant Jam, 164
  ,, ,, Jelly, 160
  ,, ,, Sauce, 45
Bread, 180
  ,, and Milk, 75
  ,, Potato, 129
  ,, Sauce, 45
  ,, Whole-meal, 180
Brocoli, 141
  ,, Greens, 141
Brown Mushroom Sauce, 55
  ,, Onion Sauce, 55

Brown Roux, 22
„ Thickening, 22
Brussels Sprouts, 141
„ „ Tinned, 154
Butter, Black, 48
„ Maître d'Hôtel, 53
„ Melted, 48
„ Oiled, 48
„ Sauce, 46

Cabbage, 142
„ and Cream, 143
„ and Rice, 63
„ large White, 142
„ Red, 143
„ Soup, 27
Cakes, 177
„ Parsnip, 147
„ Pound, 179
Caper Sauce, 49
Carrot Jam, 164
„ Sauce, 49
„ Soup, 27
Carrots, Boiled, 143
„ Fried, 144
„ Mashed, 144
„ Tinned, 154
Cauliflower and Tomato Sauce, 145
„ au gratin, 144
„ Boiled, 144
„ Salad, 104
„ Sauce, 49
„ Soup, 28
Casseroles, 64
Celery and Eggs, 85
„ Salad, 103
„ Sauce, 49
„ Soup, 29
„ Stewed, 145
Cheesecakes, 165–168
„ Almond, 170
„ Apple, 170
„ from Curds, 169
„ Orange, 170
„ Potato, 169
Cheese and Eggs, 89
„ and Fried Bread, 113
„ and Rice, 63
„ Devilled, 114
„ Fritters, 117

Cheese Ramequins, 114
„ Sandwiches, 107
„ Savoury, 113
„ Soufflé, 92
„ Soup, 29
„ Stewed, 114
„ Straws, 114
„ Toasted, 114
Cherry Sauce, 49
„ Soup, 29
Cherries, Stewed, 174
Chestnut Sauce, 49
„ Soup, 30
Chestnuts and Macaroni, 72
Chocolate Cream, 166
„ Fritters, 119
Chutney Sauce, 53
Cinnamon Sauce, 49
Clear Soup, 30
Cocoanut Sauce, 49
„ Soup, 31
Coffee Cream, 166
„ Fritters, 119
Cottage Soup, 30
Cream and Macaroni, 73
„ Cheese Sandwiches, 107
„ Chocolate, 166
„ Coffee, 166
„ Fritters, 120
„ Lemon, 166
„ Maraschino, 166
„ Orange, 166
„ Pistachio, 167
„ Strawberry, 167
„ Vanilla, 166
Creams, 165
Croquettes, Potato, 127
„ Rice, 65
Cucumber and Eggs, 88
„ Salad, 102
„ Sauce, 49
Currant Sauce, Black, 50
„ „ Red, 50
„ Black, Jam, 164
„ Black, Jelly, 160
„ Red, Jam, 164
„ Red, Jelly, 161
Curried Eggs, 82
„ Lentils, 136
„ Rice 63

INDEX. 189

Curried Vegetables, 151
Curry Sauce, 50
Custard, Apple, 168
„ Cheap, 168
„ Fritters, 119
Custards, 167
Cutlets, Potato, 127

Damson Jam, 164
„ Jelly, 162
Dandelion Salad, 103
Devilled Cheese, 114
„ Eggs, 82
Dutch Sauce, 51
„ „ Green, 51

Egg Balls, 83
„ Forcemeat, 83
„ Salad, 99
„ Sandwiches, 106
„ Sauce, 51
„ Toast, 85
Eggs, 78
„ à la bonne femme, 83
„ à la Dauphine, 85
„ à la tripe, 83
„ and Asparagus, 85
„ „ Black Butter, 86
„ „ Celery, 85
„ „ Cheese, 89
„ „ Cucumber, 88
„ „ Garlic, 86
„ „ Mushrooms, 86
„ „ Onions, 87
„ „ Potatoes, 87
„ „ Rice, 66
„ „ Sauce Robert, 87
„ „ Sorrel, 87
„ „ Spinach, 85
„ „ Turnip-tops, 85
„ au gratin, 84
„ Boiled, 78
„ „ Hard, 81
„ Broiled, 87
„ Buttered, 88
„ Curried, 82
„ Devilled, 82
„ Fried, 80
„ in Sunshine, 88
„ Little, 89

Eggs Poached, 81
„ Scrambled, 88
„ To Break, 80
Endive, 145
„ Salad, 100
„ Soup, 31
English Salad, 97
Extract of Spinach, 25

Fennel Sauce, 51
Flageolets, 133
„ Tinned, 154
Fond d'Artichokes, 155
Forcemeat of Egg, 83
„ of Mushroom, 110
Frangipane Fritters, 120
French Beans, 139
„ Bean Salad, 102
„ „ Soup, 27
„ „ Pudding, 140
„ Salad, 97
Fritters, 116
„ Almond, 119
„ Apple, 118
„ Apricot, 119
„ Banana, 119
„ Batter for, 116
„ Cheese, 117
„ Chocolate, 119
„ Coffee, 119
„ Cream, 120
„ Custard, 119
„ Frangipane, 120
„ Game, 117
„ German, 121
„ Ginger and Rice, 121
„ Hominy, 117
„ Mushroom, 116
„ Orange, 120
„ Pine Apple, 120
„ Peach, 120
„ Potato, 120
„ Rice, 121
„ Sage and Onion, 118
„ Spinach, 118
„ Sweet, 118
„ Tomato, 117
„ Vanilla, 119
Fruit, Compote of, 171
„ Soup, 31

Fruit, Stewed, 171
Fruits, Bottled, 157
,, Tinned, 155
Frumenty, 76

Game Fritters, 117
Garlic and Eggs, 86
Garnish of Eggs, 89
German Fritters, 121
,, Salad, 100
,, Sauce, 51
Ginger Sauce, 52
Gooseberry Sauce, 52
Gooseberries, Stewed, 173
Green Bean Soup, 27
,, Dutch Sauce, 51
,, Mayonnaise Sauce, 54
,, Pea Soup, Dried, 37
,, ,, ,, Fresh, 38

Hare Soup, 32
Haricot Beans, 131
,, Bean Salad, 103
,, ,, Soup, Red, 26
,, ,, ,, White, 26
Herbaceous Mixture, 32
Herbs, Aromatic, 32
Hominy, 76
,, Fried, 76
,, Fritters, 117
Hop Salad, 104
Horseradish Sauce, 52
Hotch Potch, 32

Ice Cream, 176
,, Lemon Water, 176
,, Orange Water, 176
,, Water Fruit, 177
Ices, 174
,, from Fresh Fruit, 176
,, from Jams, 176
Indian Pickle Sauce, 53
,, Sandwiches, 106
Italian Salad, 104
,, Sauce, 53

Jam Apple, 161
,, Apricot, 164
,, Blackberry, 164
,, Black Currant, 164

Jam, Carrot, 164
,, Damson, 164
,, Gooseberry, 164
,, Greengage, 164
,, Plum, 164
,, Raspberry, 164
,, Red Currant, 164
,, Rhubarb, 164
,, Strawberry, 164
,, Vegetable Marrow, 164
Jams, 163
Jardinière Soup, 33
Jellies, 158
Jelly, Apple, 161
,, Apricot, 163
,, Blackberry, 158
,, Black Currant, 160
,, Damson, 162
,, Lemon, 159
,, Mulberry, 163
,, Orange, 160
,, Pine Apple, 162
,, Raspberry, 161
,, Red Currant, 161
Julienne Soup, 33

Kale, Scotch, 148
,, Sea, 148

Leek Soup, 33
Leeks, Stewed, 145
,, Welsh Porridge, 146
Lemon Cream, 166
,, Jelly, 159
,, Water, Ice, 176
Lentil Porridge, 75
,, Purée à la Soubise, 34
,, Soup, 33
Lentils, 135
,, à la Provençale, 136
,, Boiled, 136
,, Curried, 136
Lettuce Salad, 97
Lettuces, Stewed, 146
,, with Peas, 146

Macaroni, 67
,, à la Reine, 69
,, and Cheese, 68
,, ,, Chestnuts, 72

Macaroni and Cream, 73
„ „ Eggs, 69
„ „ Tomatoes, 72
„ as an Ornament, 70
„ au gratin, 69
„ Italian Fashion, 68
„ Nudels, 71
„ Savoury, 72
„ Scolloped, 70
„ Soup, Clear, 34
„ Soup, Thick, 34
„ Timbale of, 70
Macedoines, 155
Maître d'Hôtel Sauce, 53
„ „ Butter, 53
Mango Chutney Sauce, 53
Maraschino Cream, 166
Mayonnaise Salad, 98
„ Sauce, 53
„ Sauce, Green, 54
Melon Salad, 105
Milk Porridge, 75
„ Soup, 35
„ Toast, 77
Mint Sauce, 54
Mock Turtle Soup, 35
Mulberry Jelly, 163
Mulligatawny Soup, 35
Mushroom, Essence of, 44
„ Forcemeat, 110
„ Fritters, 116
„ Pie, 110
„ „ Cold, 110
„ Pudding, 111
„ Purée of, 55
„ Sandwiches, 106
„ Sauce, 54
„ „ Brown, 55
Mushrooms, 108
„ à la Bordelaise, 110
„ à la Provencale, 110
„ and Eggs, 86
„ au gratin, 109
„ Fried, 109
„ Plain, 108
Mustard Sauce, 55
Mustard and Cress, 104
„ „ „ Sandwiches, 106

Nalesnikis, 116

Nettles, To Boil, 151

Oatmeal Porridge, 73
Oiled Butter, 48
Omelet au Kirsch, 95
„ au Rhum, 95
„ Cheese, 92
„ Fine Herbs, 92
„ Onion, 92
„ Plain, 91
„ Potato, 92
„ Potato, Sweet, 92
„ Soufflée, 93
„ Sweet, 94
„ Vegetable, 95
„ with Jam, 94
Omelets, 89
Onion Omelet, 92
„ Salad, 104
„ Sauce, 55
„ „ Brown, 55
„ Soup, 35
„ „ Brown, 36
Onions and Eggs, 87
„ Baked, 146
„ Plain, 146
„ Stewed, 147
„ Stuffed, 115
Orange Cheesecakes, 170
„ Cream, 166
„ Fritters, 120
„ Jelly, 160
„ Sauce, 56
„ Water Ice, 176
Ox-tail Soup, 36

Palestine Soup, 24
Pancakes, Polish, 116
Parsley Sauce, 56
„ To Blanch, 26
Parsnip Cake, 147
„ Soup, 36
Parsnips, 147
„ Fried, 147
„ Mashed, 147
Paste for Pies, 184.
„ „ Puddings, 185.
„ without Butter, 183.
Peach Fritters, 120
Peaches, Tinned, 156

Peaches with Cream, 156
Pea Soup, Dried Green, 37
„ „ Split Peas, 37
„ „ Fresh Green, 38
Peas, Boiled, 148
„ Brose, 134
„ Dried, 133
„ Dried Green with Cream, 135
„ Dried whole Green, 134
„ Green, 148
„ Pudding, 134
„ Stewed, 148
„ Tinned, 153
Pear Soup, 37
Pears, Stewed, 173
„ Tinned, 156
Pie, Mushroom, 110
„ Mushroom, Cold, 111
„ Potato, 112
„ Pumpkin, 113
Pies and Puddings, General, 183
„ Paste for, 184.
Pine Apple Fritters, 120
„ „ Ice, 177
„ „ Jelly, 162
„ „ Sauce, 56
„ „ Tinned, 156
Piroski Sernikis, 116
Pistachio Cream, 167
Plum Jam, 164
„ Sauce, 56
Plums, Stewed, 174
Polenta, 115
Poached Eggs, 81
Poivrade Sauce, 57
Polish Pancakes, 116
Porridge, Barley and Rice, 75
„ Milk, 75
„ Lentil, 75
„ Oatmeal, 73
„ Sago, 77
„ Whole Meal, 75
Potato Balls, 127
„ Biscuits, 129
„ Border, 128
„ Bread, 129
„ Cake, 129
„ Cheese, 130
„ Cheesecake, 169
„ Chips, 126

Potato Croquettes, 127
„ Fritters, 120
„ Omelet, 92
„ Omelet, Sweet, 92
„ Ribbon, 126
„ Salad, 101
„ Soup, 38
Potatoes and Eggs, 87
„ à la Barigoule, 130
„ à la Lyonnaise, 131
„ à la Maître d'Hôtel, 127
„ à la Provençale, 131
„ Baked, 125
„ Boiled, 123
„ Broiled, 131
„ Fried, 126
„ Mashed, 125
„ New, 127
„ Sauté, 126
„ Steamed, 124
Pound Cake, 179
Prune Sauce, 57
Prunes, Stewed, 173
Pudding, Cheese, 114
„ French Bean, 140
„ Mushroom, 111
„ Peas, 134
„ Pumpkin, 113
Puddings, 182
Pumpkin à la Parmesane, 115
„ Pie, 113
„ Pudding, 113
„ Soup, 39
Purée, Endive, 31
„ Lentils, 34
„ Mushroom, 55
„ of Beans, Red, 26
„ of Beans, White, 26
„ of Chestnuts, 30
„ Sorrel, 58

Rarebit, Welsh, 115
Raspberry Ice, 176
„ Jam, 164
„ Jelly, 161
„ Sauce, 57
Ramequins, Cheese, 114
Ratafia Sauce, 57
Ravigotte Sauce, 57
Red Currant Jam, 164

INDEX.

Red Currant Jelly, 161
,, ,, Sauce, 50
Red Haricot Bean Soup, 26
Rhubarb Soup, 39
,, Stewed, 173
Rice, 60
,, and Barley Porridge, 75
,, and Cabbage, 63
,, and Cheese, 63
,, and Eggs, 66
,, and Ginger Fritters, 121
,, and Tomatoes, 66
,, Boiled, 61
,, Border, 64
,, Croquettes, 65
,, Curried, 63
,, Fritters, 121
,, Soup, 39
,, Soup à la Royale, 39
Risotto, 62
Robert Sauce, 58
Roux, Brown, 22
,, White, 22

Sage and Onion Fritters, 118
Sago Porridge, 77
,, Soup, 40
Salad, Artichoke, 102
,, Asparagus, 101
,, Bean, Broad, 103
,, Bean, Haricot, 103
,, Beetroot, 102
,, Cauliflower, 104
,, Celery, 103
,, Cucumber, 102
,, Dandelion, 103
,, Egg, 99
,, Endive, 100
,, English, 97
,, French, 97
,, French Beans, 102
,, German, 100
,, Hop, 104
,, Italian, 104
,, Mayonnaise, 98
,, Melon, 105
,, Mixed, 98
,, Mustard and Cress, 104
,, Onion, 104
,, Potato, 101

Salad, Salsify, 101
,, Sweet, 105
,, Tomato, 99
,, Water-cress, 103
Salads, 96
Salsify, Boiled, 151
,, Salad, 101
Sandwiches, 105
,, Cheese, 107
,, Cream Cheese, 107
,, Egg, 106
,, Indian, 106
,, Mushroom, 106
,, Mustard and Cress, 107
,, Tomato, 105
Sauce, Allemande, 44
,, Almond, 44
,, Almond, Clear, 45
,, Apple, 45
,, Arrowroot, 45
,, Artichoke, 45
,, Asparagus, 45
,, Bread, 45
,, Butter, 46
,, Butter, Black, 48
,, Butter, Oiled, 48
,, Caper, 49
,, Carrot, 49
,, Cauliflower, 49
,, Celery, 49
,, Cherry, 49
,, Chestnut, 49
,, Cinnamon, 49
,, Cocoa-nut, 49
,, Cucumber, 49
,, Currant, Black, 50
,, Currant, Red, 50
,, Curry, 50
,, Dutch, 51
,, ,, Green, 51
,, Egg, 51
,, Fennel, 51
,, German Sweet, 51
,, Ginger, 52
,, Gooseberry, 52
,, Horseradish, 52
,, Indian Pickle, 53
,, Italian, 53
,, Maître d'Hôtel, 53
,, Mango Chutney, 53

Sauce, Mayonnaise, 53
,, ,, Green, 54
,, Mint, 54
,, Mushroom, 54
,, ,, Brown, 55
,, ,, Purée, 55
,, Mustard, 55
,, Onion, 55
,, ,, Brown, 55
,, Orange Cream, 56
,, Parsley, 56
,, Pine Apple, 56
,, Plum, 56
,, Poivrade, 57
,, Prune, 57
,, Radish, 57
,, Raspberry, 57
,, Ratafia, 57
,, Ravigotte, 57
,, Robert, 58
,, Sorrel, 58
,, Soubise, 58
,, Sweet, 58
,, Tarragon, 58
,, Tartar, 58
,, Tomato, 59
,, Truffle, 59
,, Vanilla, 59
,, White, 59
Sauces, 44
Savoury Rice, 66
Scotch Broth, 40
,, Kale, 148
Sea Kale, 148
,, ,, Soup, 40
Sorrel Sauce, 58
,, Soup, 40
Soubise Sauce, 58
Soufflé, Cheese, 92
,, Omelet, 93
Soup, Almond, 23
,, Apple, 24
,, Artichoke, 24
,, Asparagus, 24
,, Barley, 25
,, Bean, French, 27
,, ,, Green, 27
,, ,, Haricot, Red, 26
,, ,, Haricot, White, 26
,, Beetroot, 26

Soup, Cabbage, 27
,, Carrot, 27
,, Cauliflower, 28
,, Celery, 29
,, Cheese, 29
,, Cherry, 29
,, Chestnut, 30
,, Clear, 30
,, Cocoanut, 31
,, Cottage, 30
,, Endive, 31
,, Fruit, 31
,, Green Pea, Dried, 37
,, ,, ,, Fresh, 38
,, Hare, 32
,, Hotch Potch, 32
,, Jardinière, 33
,, Julienne, 33
,, Leek, 33
,, Lentil, 33
,, Lentil à la Soubise, 34
,, Macaroni, Clear, 34
,, ,, Thick, 34
,, Milk, 35
,, Mock Turtle, 35
,, Mulligatawny, 35
,, Onion, 35
,, ,, Brown, 36
,, Ox-tail, 36
,, Palestine, 24
,, Parsnip, 36
,, Pear, 37
,, Pea, Split, 37
,, ,, Green, Dried, 37
,, ,, ,, Fresh, 38
,, Potato, 38
,, Pumpkin, 39
,, Rhubarb, 39
,, Rice, 39
,, ,, à la Royale, 39
,, Sago, 40
,, Scotch Broth, 40
,, Sea Kale, 40
,, Sorrel, 40
,, Spinach, 41
,, Tapioca, 41
,, Tomato, 41
,, Turnip, 42
,, Vegetable, 33
,, ,, Marrow, 42

Soup, Vermicelli, 42
" " White, 42
" White, 43
Soups, 23
" General Instructions, 17
Sparghetti, 67
Spinach, 149
" and Eggs, 85
" Extract of, 25
" Fritters, 118
" Soup, 41
" Tinned, 154
Stock, 21
Strawberry Cream, 167
" Ice, 176
" Jam, 164
Sweet Fritters, 118
" Omelet, 94
" Salads, 105
" Sauce, 58
" " German, 51

Tagliatelli, 73
Tapioca Soup, 41
Tarragon Sauce, 58
Tartar Sauce, 58
Thickening, Brown, 22
" White, 22
Timbale of Macaroni, 70
Toast, Egg, 85
" Milk, 77
Tomato Fritters, 117
" Pie, 112
" Salad, 99
" Sandwiches, 105
" Sauce, 59
" Soup, 41
Tomatoes and Macaroni, 72
" and Rice, 66
" au Gratin, 111
" Baked, 111

Tomatoes, Fried, 111
" Grilled, 111
" Stewed, 111
Truffle Sauce, 59
Turnip Soup, 42
" -tops, 151
" " and Eggs, 85
Turnips, Boiled, 150
" Mashed, 150
" Ornamental, 150
" Tinned, 155

Vanilla Cream, 166
" Fritters, 119
" Ice, 176
" Sauce, 59
Vegetable Curry, 151
" Marrow, 149
" " Soup, 42
" " Stuffed, 149
" Omelet, 95
" Soup, 42
Vegetables, Fresh, 137
" Preserved, 152
" Substantial, 122
Vermicelli Soup, 42
" " Thick, 42

Water-cress Salad, 103
Welsh Porridge, 146
" Rarebit, 115
White Haricot Bean Salad, 103
" " " Soup, 26
" Roux, 22
" Sauce, 59
" Soup, 43
" Thickening, 22
Whole-meal Bread, 180
" " Porridge, 75

Zucchetti Farcis, 115

PRINTED BY
CASSELL & COMPANY, LIMITED, LA BELLE SAUVAGE,
LONDON, E.C.

www.ingramcontent.com/pod-product-compliance
Lightning Source LLC
Chambersburg PA
CBHW020839160426
43192CB00007B/719